Feel Free to Say It

Feel Free to Say It

Threats to Freedom of Speech in Britain Today

Philip Johnston

Civitas: Institute for the Study of Civil Society
London

First Published March 2013

© Civitas 2013
55 Tufton Street
London SW1P 3QL

email: books@civitas.org.uk

All rights reserved

ISBN 978-1-906837-50-1

Independence: Civitas: Institute for the Study of Civil Society is a registered educational charity (No. 1085494) and a company limited by guarantee (No. 04023541). Civitas is financed from a variety of private sources to avoid over-reliance on any single or small group of donors.

Typeset by
Civitas

Printed in Great Britain by
Berforts Group Ltd
Stevenage SG1 2BH

Contents

Author

Philip Johnston is assistant editor, leader writer and an award-winning weekly columnist of the *Daily Telegraph*. He was previously the newspaper's home affairs editor and chief political correspondent. He is the author of *Bad Laws* (Constable and Robinson, 2010).

Foreword

We used to be proud that every British citizen enjoyed freedom of speech. We didn't need a 'first amendment' — the right to speak freely was ingrained in our institutional genes. And we knew why the freedom to speak without fear or favour is important—the truth is more likely to emerge. Even if some people found criticism upsetting, free speech was a public benefit that vastly exceeded the importance of mere hurt feelings.

An exception has long been made for remarks intended to frighten people. In the 1930s, for example, fascist gangs marched through the East End of London chanting words and displaying banners intended to frighten Jews who lived locally. The 1936 Public Order Act rightly made it illegal to put people in fear of death or injury. But we have come a long way from this reasonable limit on free speech. Some of our police have become less like protectors of the weak and more like vigilantes actively seeking occasions when they can use the law to silence individuals.

Possibly the most absurd recent case concerned a Czech woman who got into a row with a neighbour in Macclesfield. Petra Mills was found guilty of racially abusing her New Zealand-born neighbour by calling her a 'stupid, fat, Australian bitch'. The neighbour was from New Zealand and, like all self-respecting New Zealanders, hates to be confused with Australians. The judge commented that: 'The word Australian was used. It was racially aggravated and the main reason it was used was in hostility.' A fine of £110 was imposed for a racially-aggravated offence. Legally, calling her a fat bitch would

ix

have been fine, but the national epithet made it a hate crime.

Philip Johnston describes the legal atmosphere we now face and puts it in its historical context, revealing just how far we have fallen from our longstanding liberal ideals.

David G. Green

The liberty of speaking and writing... guards our other liberties.

Thomas Jefferson

Preface

Exactly 250 years ago, on 23 April 1763, the rabble-rousing MP John Wilkes published Number 45 of his radical newsletter *The North Briton*, and triggered one of the great battles over free speech that resonates to this day. Wilkes is largely forgotten in this country yet remains something of a folk hero in the United States because of his influence on the Founding Fathers of the republic and in particular their commitment to free expression.

By all accounts, Wilkes was a distinctly unpleasant individual. He was a member of the Knights of St Francis of Wycombe, otherwise known as the Hellfire Club or the Monks of Medmenham Abbey. This group made the Bullingdon at Oxford, to which Boris Johnson and David Cameron belonged, seem like the Mothers' Union. It was renowned for its debauchery, anti-Catholic ribaldry, and orgies with women dressed as nuns and members in Franciscan robes.

It was Wilkes who, when told by the Earl of Sandwich that 'you will die either on the gallows, or of the pox,' replied with the immortal line: 'That must depend on whether I embrace your lordship's principles or your mistress.'

Wilkes is very much an eighteenth-century figure yet he remains relevant today because we appear to be just as confused now as we were then about what we can say and who, if anyone, should control it. Unlike Wilkes, whose pamphlets would have been read by relatively few people, we live in a world with myriad outlets for public expression and a seemingly indefatigable desire to use them. We also live in a time when it is becoming increasingly difficult to give offence, even unwittingly, without facing either prosecution or persecution.

Wilkes was happy to give offence; indeed he revelled in doing so and as a consequence became a martyr to free speech, albeit a reluctant one. He was elected to the House of Commons in 1757 by the time-honoured rotten borough method of bribing voters; but any hopes he had of early office were dashed when the government of William Pitt the Elder, the first Earl of Chatham, fell.

Wilkes spent his time developing a fine line in parliamentary putdowns and ridicule that brought him admirers and enemies in equal number. His principle target was John Stuart, the Earl of Bute and prime minister from 1760, when George III came to the throne. Bute was an early believer in 'getting your message across' and hired a spin doctor in the shape of Tobias Smollett, the novelist and historian, to edit a government-friendly paper, *The Briton*.

This was Wilkes's chance to spread his disdain for Bute's administration beyond Parliament to a wider audience, and within a week he and a friend Charles Churchill began the anonymous publication of a rival newsletter, *The North Briton*. This was the *Private Eye* of its day, only without the latter's customary restraint or attention to facts. Insults, scandal and rumour were its stock in trade, with attacks on senior members of the Establishment that were extraordinary for the time even if now they might feature in the leader columns of the average newspaper.

Lord Egremont was 'a weak, passionate, and insolent secretary of state,' and Secretary of the Treasury Samuel Martin was 'the most treacherous, base, selfish, mean, abject, low-lived and dirty fellow, that ever wriggled himself into a secretaryship.' Baiting Bute, however, remained Wilkes's favourite sport. He dragged up a salacious rumour that Bute was in a sexual relationship with the King's mother. Just to drive the image home, *The North Briton* No. 5 included the story of Roger de Mortimer, the manipulative regent during Edward III's minority, who was the lover of the Queen Mother Isabella. Wilkes then published an edition of an old play, *The Fall of Mortimer*, with a satirical dedication to Bute: 'History does not furnish a more striking contrast than there is between the two ministers in the reigns of Edward the Third and George the Third'.

Every week, *The North Briton* piled the abuse on Bute and, to add insult to injury, Wilkes's pamphlet easily outsold the government's insipid newsletter by ten copies to one. As Charles Chevenix Trench observed, 'Wilkes made Bute the most hated Minister the country had known.'[1]

Wilkes's invective eventually helped propel Bute from office early in 1763 and *The North Briton* ceased publication for a while, but not for long. On 13 April, Wilkes was back with the question: 'The SCOTTISH minister has indeed retired. Is HIS influence at an end?' *North Briton* No. 45 carried a sustained attack on the King's Speech for the new Parliament unlike anything seen before, even if it might look somewhat unexceptionable today. Wilkes's offence was to couch what appeared to be an attack on George III as though it were a denunciation of his ministry.

He began: 'This week has given the public the most abandoned instance of ministerial effrontery ever attempted to be imposed on mankind. The minister's speech of last Tuesday is not to be paralleled in the annals of this country. I am in doubt, whether the imposition is greater on the sovereign or on the nation. Every friend of his country must lament that a prince of so many great and amiable qualities, whom England truly reveres, can be brought to give the sanction of his sacred name to the most odious measures, and to the most unjustifiable public declarations, from a throne ever renowned for truth, honour, and unsullied virtue.'

If this looks a bit tame by modern standards it caused outrage. Wilkes had crossed the line that we still have difficulty identifying today between what is and is not acceptable. Then it was widely accepted that the monarch was above reproach, so Wilkes was arrested and charged with seditious libel intended to turn public opinion against the king. A general warrant was issued that led to the arrest of 49 others, many of them innocent parties, and Wilkes ran rings around the authorities, claiming parliamentary privilege and exposing gaping holes in their procedures

There then began a series of trials to consider the legal questions, which gave Wilkes the chance to make even more of a splash. His prosecution, he said, would 'determine at once whether English liberty be a reality or a shadow.' The Court of Common Pleas agreed, quashed the catch-all warrant and ruled Wilkes exempt from prosecution. This was an extraordinary blow for liberty and free speech against what had until then been an almost despotic system.

Wilkes became a hero of the Founding Fathers of the United States of America, where he is remembered today more than here. Or at least his success in facing down the establishment was considered heroic if not his person. To Benjamin Franklin, Wilkes was 'an outlaw... of bad personal character, not worth a farthing'. The free speech provisions in the US constitution and several subsequent rulings of the American courts cite the Wilkes case; yet in his native land he is largely forgotten.

Wilkes was a pretty loathsome individual saying pretty loathsome things about some pretty loathsome people. Since they happened to be senior officers of the state they were considered fair game. But can free speech be exercised to the point where it is considered abusive only when it is deployed against government ministers? If the term means anything then surely it must involve the liberty to say anything about any subject without being arrested or tried—provided it does not trigger violence. Is it right to protect the feelings of particular groups of people by suppressing the rights of others to say what they think about them? We now have a plethora of laws ranging from hate crimes to public order offences that circumscribe free expression. Those who do not like them argue that people should just toughen up and accept that living in a free country means running the risk of being abused. On the other hand, is not a civilised country one that prevents minorities being the target for invective and disdain? Why should immigrants have no redress if they are told to 'go back to where you came from'? Should a gay person be protected by the law from the views of those who think homosexuality is a sin? Clearly, most people want neither a free-for-all (though some do) or total proscription. There is a balance to be struck. The question is: have we got it right?

Introduction

On 14 January 2013, Theresa May, the Home Secretary, told the House of Commons that the Government was prepared to change the law to stop an insult being a crime. After a lengthy campaign by free speech activists, she announced that an amendment made by the House of Lords to the Crime and Courts Bill would no longer be contested. As a result, the word 'insulting' would be removed from the offence of using threatening, abusive or insulting words or behaviour in Section 5 of the Public Order Act 1986. 'There is always a careful balance to be struck between protecting our proud tradition of free speech and taking action against those who cause widespread offence with their actions,' May said.

So did this announcement really ensure that 'a careful balance' had been struck? Was it, as campaigners asserted, a 'victory for free speech'; or do we remain as confused as ever about what that entails?

A clue was provided by what the Home Secretary said next: 'The Government support the retention of Section 5 as it currently stands, because we believe that the police should be able to take action when they are sworn at, when protesters burn poppies on Armistice Day and in similar scenarios.'

She added: 'Looking at past cases, the Director of Public Prosecutions could not identify any where the behaviour leading to a conviction could not be described as "abusive" as well as "insulting". He has stated that the word "insulting" could safely be removed without the risk of undermining the ability of the CPS to bring prosecutions. On that basis, the Government are not minded to challenge the amendment made in the other place. We will issue guidance to the police on the range of powers that remain available to them to deploy in the kind of situation I described, but the word "insulting" should be removed from Section 5.'

In other words, it did not matter that the word insulting was being removed from the Public Order Act because the statute's other provisions would still allow the police to arrest people on the same basis as before — for expressing views that might be considered offensive but which in a free country they should have the right to express.

Simon Calvert, director of the Reform Section 5 campaign said: 'This is a victory for free speech. People of all shades of opinion have suffered at the hands of Section 5. By accepting the Lords amendment to reform it the Government has managed to please the widest possible cross-section of society. They have done the right thing and we congratulate them.'

Yet in view of the caveats attached to May's announcement, the celebrations of campaigners were almost certainly misplaced. After all, they had been pressing for the removal of the word 'insulting' from the 1986 Act because it had been used, *inter alia*, against two Christian hoteliers who took issue with a guest over the religious requirements of Islam and to prosecute a street preacher who questioned the morality of homosexuality.

However, as the Home Secretary acknowledged, the change in the law would not prevent similar cases either leading to arrest or being brought before the courts. It might not result in a conviction but that is not the point. An arrest, even if the individual is released without charge within hours, is of itself an infringement of free speech, as well as being deeply traumatic. So, too, is waiting weeks or months for a case to be heard in court, even if the hearing results in an acquittal. The prospect of a trial inevitably entails anguish and is often accompanied by other consequences such as a loss of business or dismissal from a job. We tend to forget how often this statute is used. Official figures show that the number of proceedings average 25,000 a year, with half ending in conviction.[1]

The Government was commended for having listened to the calls for insults to be made lawful once more. But ministers were not motivated by a desire to protect free speech: they had not wanted to make this concession and were forced to do so by a defeat in the Lords and the prospect of another in the Commons.

In any case, the threat to free speech goes far wider than anything addressed by May's statement. On the same day that she made the concession, the *Observer* newspaper took down a column from its website by the polemical writer Julie Burchill because it was deemed offensive to transsexuals. Burchill had written the piece in support of another journalist, Suzanne Moore, who had come under attack on Twitter for suggesting in a *New Statesman* article that women were too often expected to look like 'a Brazilian transsexual'. Moore then said she was quitting the social networking site because of the abuse she had received, which included being accused of being a fascist.

In her column, Burchill wrote of transgender people as 'screaming mimis', 'bed-wetters in bad wigs' and 'dicks in chicks' clothing'. She added that 'the very vociferous transsexual lobby and their grim groupies' reminded her of 'wretched inner-city kids who shoot another inner-city kid dead in a fast-food shop for not showing them

3

enough "respect"'. She also compared the attacks on Moore to 'the Black and White Minstrels telling Usain Bolt how to run'.

Burchill's column attracted hundreds of hostile comments and even prompted a Government minister to demand her dismissal from the *Observer*, for what she described as 'a bigoted vomit'. It is noteworthy that those who consider themselves to be on the 'right' side of such a controversy believe they are fully entitled to deploy abusive language to denounce people whose rhetoric has often been more restrained than that of their critics.

Blinded by self-righteousness, they seem unable to understand that their freedom to fulminate against a perceived offence must be balanced by the right of an individual to give that offence in the first place. When government ministers start to demand the dismissal of people for expressing views that are not considered 'acceptable' then we really have moved a long way from the 'careful balance' sought by Theresa May.

What made this affair especially worrying was the way the *Observer* reacted. The editor John Mulholland ordered the article taken off the paper's website, though the nature of the internet made this little more than a craven gesture since it was available in many other places.

Mulholland tried to justify his action: 'The *Observer* is a paper which prides itself on ventilating difficult debates and airing challenging views. On this occasion we got it wrong and in light of the hurt and offence caused I apologise.'[2]

This was an extraordinary thing to do. As Toby Young wrote on the *Telegraph* website: 'Whatever you think of its politics, the *Observer* is a paper with a great liberal tradition. For it to muzzle one of its own journalists—

4

albeit a freelance contributor—on the grounds that some people on the Left found her views distasteful is a betrayal of everything the paper is supposed to stand for.'[3]

He added: 'Why does he [Mulholland] think the paper "got it wrong" on this occasion? Because the article caused "offence"? It cannot be said often enough that freedom of speech, if it means anything, must include the freedom to say things that some people find offensive... At a time when Fleet Street is engaged in an existential battle to protect free speech from political interference [after the Leveson inquiry] Mulholland's act is grossly irresponsible.'

If a national newspaper editor is not going to defend the right of his writers to express a contrarian, even offensive, view then why should the police and the DPP bother? It is, of course, up to the editor what goes in his newspaper and on his website. Editors often spike articles on grounds of taste; but this one was 'de-published' because it attracted criticism from a particular quarter, the gender equality industry that brooks no criticism from anyone on any grounds. We will hear a good deal more from them as the debate over gay marriage unfolds.

Take the case of Adam Smith, a Christian housing worker who in February 2011 posted a link to an article from the BBC News website on his Facebook page. The headline was 'Gay church marriages get go ahead' and Smith, 55, added the comment, 'an equality too far'. Two colleagues read the remark, which could be viewed by friends and friends of friends, and one of them posted a response asking Mr Smith to explain what he meant. The next evening he posted: 'I don't understand why people who have no faith and don't believe in Christ would want to get hitched in church. The Bible is quite specific that marriage is for men and women. If the state wants to offer civil marriage to the same sex then that is up to the state; but the state shouldn't impose its rules on places of faith and conscience.'

For making these comments, Smith lost his managerial position, had his salary cut by 40 per cent and was given a final written warning by Manchester's Trafford Housing Trust. He was reinstated after taking the trust to an employment tribunal but what was interesting was the justification given by his employers for their action. He had broken a code of conduct by expressing religious or political views which might upset co-workers.

It is, of course, understandable that an employer will want harmony rather than discord in the office. But we have come a long way in a very short time if it is considered worthy of disciplinary action to assert that marriage is an institution involving a man and a woman.

After the hearing Smith said: 'I didn't do this for the money—I did this because there is an important principle at stake. Britain is a free country where people have freedom of speech, and I am pleased that the judge's ruling underlines that important principle. Something has poisoned the atmosphere in Britain, where an honest man like me can be punished for making perfectly polite remarks about the importance of marriage.'

Smith added: 'I have won today. But what will tomorrow bring?' What indeed?

1

The Retreat of Free Speech

More people are being jailed or arrested in Britain today for what they think, believe and say than at any time since the eighteenth century. They are not dissidents taking on an over-mighty state; nor are they courageous individuals risking their lives by speaking out against injustice in an autocratic land. Most of them would know little of the great battles for freedom of expression down the centuries and might vaguely have heard of Socrates or Wilkes or Sakharov.

The predicament in which they have found themselves is entirely unwitting; they are not martyrs to free speech but the victims of a modern confusion over what it entails. They are often working class, poorly educated individuals with an antediluvian dislike for ethnic minorities or an animus against immigrants. But they include devout Christians and Muslims, whose religious beliefs have led them to express opinions in public that are judged to be inappropriate and contrary to new laws designed to make people conform to a set of acceptable views, whether they be about religion, race or sexuality.

In a more diverse society, is it right that we should have laws that seek to suppress the opinions of minorities, however odious the majority might find them, or vice versa? Since abusive and insulting words aimed at individuals can be hurtful and traumatic, does a civilised society ensure they cannot be uttered or should it uphold the rights to freedom of expression in all circumstances?

More to the point, should the criminal law have any locus in what is essentially a matter of decent behaviour and good manners? When it does, the police and the courts become arbiters of what is right thinking rather than right behaviour.

The introduction into the UK of 'hate laws' is relatively recent, though they have existed in many European countries for years, notably the law against denying the Holocaust. America has hate laws but its First Amendment also protects free speech, so there is a balance that is lacking in Britain. Here in the UK we are taking the European road rather than the American even though it was our traditions that were taken across the Atlantic. Is it too late to turn back? Do we even want to?

The Leveson Inquiry into press ethics gave a new impetus to the free speech debate; a subject that a few years ago rarely featured in the media is now once again being debated with increasing urgency. Leaders in national newspapers about the dangers of statutory regulation, special editions of magazines such as the *Spectator* devoted to free speech and BBC programmes such as *The Moral Maze* dedicated to the subject point to a growing sense of unease that the concept most of us would associate with what it means to be a free country is under threat once more. A Free Speech Debate website established by the journalist Timothy Garton Ash has attracted widespread participation from those who fear the concept is being undermined and by those who consider these concerns to be exaggerated.

The debate is complicated by the explosion of social media websites and the ease with which opinions and comments can be disseminated to a wide audience with a greater likelihood that someone will be offended and demand redress. Indeed, some of those arrested and jailed have posted their views on Twitter or have had them vicariously broadcast on YouTube, whereupon others who were never the intended recipients or target for an abusive message have complained to the police. The way our laws are currently framed, proxy offence can land someone in jail.

There are some who believe this is how it should be. Jeremy Waldron, an English legal academic at New York University, has challenged the liberalism of his adopted country for allowing anyone to say anything about anyone. In his book, *The Harm in Hate Speech*, he argues that prohibitions of the sort we now have in the UK are important for social cohesion in a multi-ethnic and multi-racial society.

Waldron believes the Americans have overprotected speech to the detriment of good community relations and decency. He also observes that it is usually a liberal bystander, rather than the target of hate speech, who is most willing to defend the rights of the offending speaker. But what he must also consider, too, is that often a bystander rather than the target who is the complainant.

In any case, there have always been laws in the UK that proscribe free speech if its exercise is likely to lead to a breach of the peace. What we have seen introduced in the past 15 years are laws that constrain the expression of opinions because some people may not like them. They do not even need to be especially traumatised but merely feel aggrieved.

This is not really about free speech at all, but about setting the parameters for the decent treatment of all members of society. But in that case, should it be a matter for the criminal law at all? If we are concerned primarily with the social policing of behaviour is that not better achieved through exhortation and general public disapproval than by sending people to jail?

It is interesting to see this matter addressed in the United States, a country where free speech is enshrined in the constitution and where it has long been accepted that tolerating hateful speech is better than introducing codes and controls that might threaten the expression of unpopular ideas.

Here in Britain those fears have been realised. As Josie Appleton of the libertarian Manifesto Club observed:

> Hate speech is different to the old common-law crime of incitement, or encouraging or pressuring another person to commit a crime. Where the 'harm' of incitement is related to an actual or potential criminal act, the harm of hate speech is in the realm of ideas: it is expression that 'incites' or 'stirs up' hatred, and lowers the standing of a group in public esteem. Hate speech convictions are convictions of people who didn't actually do anything: they didn't attack anyone, or threaten or plan to attack anyone, or deny anyone access to services. Nor are they convictions of people whose hateful publications have large audiences or a sway over public opinion.[1]

Appleton examines the three 'hate' offences on the Statute Book—stirring up racial hatred, stirring up religious hatred, and stirring up hatred on the grounds of sexual orientation—and finds 'that the small number of individuals prosecuted under them are sad, marginal types, with relatively limited effect on anything or anybody.' She adds: 'It often appears that their hateful speech was a consequence of this social marginalisation.'[2]

But educated liberals can say this because they are never going to be the target of sustained abuse and, if they are, they can shrug it off. This needs to be an argument that rises above a purely functional one of protecting individuals from being upset or offended. The point about free speech is that once the state has been able to constrain it for one, apparently benign, purpose it becomes easier to restrict it further in order to close down debate or cut off dissent. The arguments in favour of doing so are deceptively attractive to right-thinking people who want to see minorities treated decently and are appalled by the abuse they have to endure.

The deception lies in what can be lost by using the criminal law to force people to conform to a particular set of beliefs expressed in a way deemed acceptable to the majority. Perversely, among those who are potentially the victims of such laws are people who now find themselves in a minority, such as devout Christians. When Labour's laws criminalising hate speech on grounds of religion and sexuality were going through Parliament they were amended to include free speech protections so that only the most offensive language or behaviour should result in prosecution.

However, other, broader, laws are also used for the same purpose, especially Section 5 of the Public Order Act, which criminalises 'threatening, abusive or insulting words or behaviour' in the vicinity of a person 'likely to be caused harassment, alarm or distress thereby'; and the Communications Act 2003, which prohibits sending 'by means of a public electronic communications network a message or other matter that is grossly offensive or of an indecent, obscene or menacing character'.

The impact of these laws and the way they are being used—or abused—is dealt with later.

2

The Trial of Socrates

But to begin with, the free speech debate should be put in a brief historical context to understand that this is not just a bit of legal tidying up but a potential threat to the defining principle of a free society. It is a principle that has been argued over and debated since the time of the ancient Greeks. Freedom of expression has always been an indispensable condition of what it means to be a free person. The first known martyr to the principle of free speech was Socrates. In 399BC he was tried before a jury in the city state of Athens for corrupting the morals of Greek youth and said he would rather be convicted than suffer restrictions on his free speech. 'If you offered to let me off this time on condition that I am not any longer to speak my mind in this search for wisdom, and that if I am caught doing this again I shall die, I should say to you, "Men of Athens, I shall obey the God rather than you. While I have life and strength I shall never cease to follow philosophy and to exhort and persuade any one of you whom I happen to meet. For this, be assured the God commands..." And, Athenians, I should go on to say, "Either acquit me or not; but understand that I shall never act differently, even if I have to die for it many times."' Oddly enough, according to the accounts of Plato and Xenophon, Socrates did not conduct his defence on what we would today consider free speech grounds. He never invoked the principle itself not least because he was not a supporter of the democratic basis of Athenian society.

Rather he engaged his prosecutors in arguments about atheism and philosophy.

In his book *The Trial of Socrates*, Izzy Stone offers an alternative line of defence that might have achieved his acquittal.

> You are not prosecuting me for any unlawful or impious act against our city or its altars. No evidence of any sort has been brought against me. You are not prosecuting me for anything I did but for what I have said and taught…Your freedom of speech is based on the assumption that every man's opinion is of value and that the many are better guides than the few. But how can you boast of your free speech if you suppress mine?
>
> The test of truly free speech is not whether what is said or taught conforms to any rule or ruler, few or many. Even under the worst dictator it is not forbidden to agree with him. It is the freedom to disagree that is freedom of speech.[1]

This, in a nutshell, is the conventional case for free speech: the right of all citizens, be they high or low, to say what they think without being locked away for doing so. Yet in the 2,300 years since Socrates, precious few societies have practised it.

Even in modern, enlightened western countries we have never been completely free to say what we like, though the reasons given for restricting free speech have often been specious. Most of us have come to accept that possessing the freedom to speak carries with it a responsibility to use it sensibly. Nor are we entirely free to insult or vilify someone. Until relatively recently there were no criminal restrictions on insults; but the opportunity for redress has long existed in the civil courts under the laws of slander and libel. These do not amount to a ban on free expression but a constraint: you can say something that might damage the reputation of another but there might be consequences if what you have said is wrong. We must accept that someone who has been the target of a calumny should be allowed to put that right in the courts. As Othello says:

> Who steals my purse steals trash; 'tis something, nothing;
> 'Twas mine, 'tis his, and has been slave to thousands;
> But he that filches from me my good name
> Robs me of that which not enriches him,
> And makes me poor indeed.

(Act III, Scene 3)

The law of libel in England has undergone many changes in the past and is about to be overhauled again, principally to reduce the exorbitant costs involved. But it is with the criminal law that this short book wishes to grapple because it is here that the threat to free speech can once again be found. We have long accepted that laws limiting free speech may be justified on public order grounds. For many people it may even be just about acceptable to criminalise a hateful rant if the person against whom it is aimed is so mortified that it amounts to an assault.

However, we have arrived at the point where an outburst of admittedly bile-filled invective is criminalised even though the target has not complained. On two occasions in recent months, women on public transport have been reported to the police, prosecuted and jailed when their words have been put on YouTube and not as a direct result of complaints made at the time. On that basis, what would stop an action being brought against Warren Mitchell for a repeat of the 1960s sitcom *Till Death Us Do Part*? His character Alf Garnett, a bigoted Cockney, differs from the two women prosecuted only in the vehemence of their racist fulminations. And if you think that is fanciful, consider that the BBC is censoring an episode of *Fawlty Towers* because the major who lives at the hotel makes racist comments, which is, of course, the point about the social satire. Most of that particular episode was taken up with Basil Fawlty's bravura and concussion-induced rail against the Germans. Will that be censored next? So where do we draw the line; indeed, should we draw a line at all?

Imagine a world where it was necessary to possess a government licence before being able to publish anything. Perhaps it does not require a great suspension of disbelief when the ethics of the press have been discussed in the minutest detail at the Leveson inquiry. Lord Justice Leveson was at pains from the outset to say he did not wish to see statutory control of the media. His view was backed by politicians who averred their passionate enthusiasm for free speech. It is astonishing that they should even need to deny the ambition. The very idea that a state licence should be required before voicing an opinion is so inimical to any concept of a free society that even contemplating the idea to reject it represents a step into the dark ages. Doubtless those who have been on the wrong end of a critical newspaper story may wish to disagree. Judging by the response to the phone-hacking scandal, there were a good number of people, including politicians, who saw what amounted to criminal behaviour as merely the most extreme manifestation of the pernicious curiosity and infernal prying of the press. For all the protestations of belief in the rights of a free media voiced at the inquiry the undertow of debate was about control and how it could be exercised, not by licensing but by the methods of redress for those who felt unjustly harmed.

The arguments over press control date back hundreds of years. In 1644, John Milton published his pamphlet *Areopagitica*, a plea to Parliament during the Civil War for the right to unlicensed printing. Milton, who had himself been subject to censorship, did not argue that anything could be said or written without consequences. The point he was making was about censorship—shutting down the argument before it had even been made. While the Greeks and Romans burned writings considered blasphemous or seditious and punished their authors, they did not stop them from writing down their thoughts. There was no licensing system of the sort that Milton faced, where a state apparatchik would determine whether an opinion was sound or not before it could get into print, something familiar to anyone who lived in one of Europe's twentieth-century tyrannies. Yes, said Milton—reject a text if you want but let it be examined first before it is condemned, not prohibited before its ideas have even been expressed. He concluded: 'Give me the liberty to know, to utter, and to argue freely according to conscience, above all liberties.'

However, as the late sceptical philosopher Richard Webster has pointed out, Milton was not quite the paragon of free speech that we often credit him for being today. *Areopagitica* is certainly a defence of freedom of the press but is also 'simultaneously a plea for maintaining a particular kind of religious intolerance'.[2]

By the time we get to the French philosopher Voltaire, we are less in the realms of moral ambivalence. In Voltaire's view, not merely was censorship wrong, but once a tract has been examined and its contents refuted, in a free country the expression of an opinion would still be allowed, however odious it may be. Voltaire is often credited with saying: 'I disapprove of what you say but I will defend to the death your right to say it.' The exact quotation is not found in his writings but that is the gist of what he meant as set out in 1906 by Evelyn Beatrice Hall in the biography *The Friends of Voltaire*.

An amalgam of Milton's and Voltaire's attitude to free speech is the golden thread running through any concept of liberty: the right to speak your mind, even if it offends other people, must be upheld. John Stuart Mill in his essay *On Liberty* took this one step further when he wrote that we must be concerned not just with the right of people to speak freely, but also to hear freely. Yet even countries that would consider themselves free and enlightened do not observe this concept. Several European states, for well-known historical reasons, have made it an offence to deny that the Holocaust happened. This is a crime in Germany, Austria and several other EU countries that were complicit in the Holocaust. Other countries, such as France, have even wider laws making it an offence to deny genocides like the Armenian massacres of 1917. Voltaire must be spinning in his grave.

It seems inconceivable that we could have such a law here in Britain. We consider people like the historian David Irvine—jailed in Austria for disputing the mass murder of Jews during WW2—as a barmy eccentric whose opinion is clearly wrong and provably so. If Irvine wants to continue ploughing his lonely ideological furrow, then let him, since his position is refuted by overwhelming evidence that what he denies actually occurred. Just leave it there.

It is unfortunate that martyrs to free speech can often be the least pleasant of individuals uttering the ghastliest calumnies—but that is precisely the point Voltaire was making. And if you think this is nothing for us to concern ourselves about, consider this: in January 1997, Tony Blair said that he might consider introducing just such a law. 'There is a very strong case that denial of the Holocaust should be a specific offence,' he told an audience in London at the opening of an exhibition devoted to the diarist Anne Frank. 'This will stand alongside our commitment to strengthen the laws against incitement to racial hatred.'[3] The irony of making such a pledge, even one that would never be fulfilled, at a commemoration to a victim of Nazism seemed lost on Mr Blair. A Labour MP, Mike Gapes, went so far as to introduce a private member's Bill into parliament to make denial of the Holocaust an offence punishable by a prison term. In 2002, the European Commission put forward a proposal for an offence of 'public denial or trivialisation of the crimes dealt with by the international military tribunal established in 1945'. Britain objected and it never went ahead but xenophobia is one of 32 extraditable crimes under the European Arrest Warrant (EAW). So although Irvine ended up in prison because he went to Austria, it is possible for someone to be removed from this country to stand trial elsewhere for expressing an unapproved opinion.

This nearly happened to Gerald Toben, an Australian academic arrested on a plane at Heathrow Airport in 2008 at the request of German authorities for publishing 'anti-Semitic and/or revisionist' material. The warrant alleged that he denied, approved or played down the mass murder of Jews perpetrated by the Nazis during the

Second World War. Even though EAW's are supposed to be implemented almost automatically and with the minimum of fuss, Toben's extradition was blocked by Westminster Magistrates Court. But this was not in some great Miltonesque defence of free speech but because the warrant contained insufficient detail about the offences.

As Toben himself said, his arrest and extradition should not have been blocked on technical grounds but because 'it's not British law, where the individual still has freedoms'.[4]

This is the conventional view of this country's position but is it any longer the case? While we may pride ourselves on being liberal enough not have a specific offence of holocaust denial, we have none the less developed a raft of laws, like a ban on 'hate speech', that limit free speech in pretty much the same way. How have we let this happen?

It has come about for reasons that are easy to understand but that does not make it any less pernicious. Supporters of holocaust denial laws say that those who perpetuate the myth that it did not take place or not to the extent widely accepted are really anti-Semites whose views can inspire violence against Jews. The orthodoxy now is that since this can be true of all minorities, all forms of racial and religious hatred should be actively prosecuted. But while that might be true when it involves violence against individuals for whatever reason, should it extend to an opinion? If someone wants to argue that all Muslims should be deported are they entitled to express that view, however odious? And in a free society, this must cut both ways. If Muslim extremists stand and jeer at British troops returning from Afghanistan, should they not be free to do so? Yet when seven radical Islamists did precisely that in 2009 they were arrested and put on trial accused of 'being abusive' under public order laws. They had shouted 'Go to hell!' and waved placards saying 'Butchers of Basra' and 'Baby killers' at British soldiers at a homecoming parade in Luton. One of the great ironies of this case was that their lawyer cited Voltaire. She told the court: 'If you believe in freedom of speech, you have to accept that some things will be said that you will like, and some things will be said that you will not like.' Indeed so, but it did not prevent the court finding the men guilty of 'causing harassment and distress'. They were given two-year conditional discharges and ordered to pay £500 in costs. What have we come to when radical Islamists, who doubtless favour a society in which free speech is non-existent, can call in aid one of the Enlightenment's great figures to remind us of our liberal bearings?

Brendan O'Neill, in a characteristically trenchant observation for the on-line magazine *Spiked*, said the case had demonstrated 'how confused and fluid' the legacy of the Enlightenment has become. 'The Islamists in Luton can be seen as taunting the rulers and thinkers of Western society, holding up Voltaire as a way of upbraiding us over our failure to adhere to the principles and attitude of the Enlightenment.'[5] The magistrates at Luton were not, of course, ignorant of the prescriptions of free speech but they felt the protestors had 'overstepped the mark'. But what is that mark? Do we know it when we see it? Is it something arbitrarily laid down by the state, the courts or by society that moves around from generation to generation? As I asked above, why is there a mark at all? In the Luton case, the district judge said the demonstrators had expressed an opinion on a matter of public interest, but had done so in 'words that amounted to being disproportionate and unreasonable.' But disproportionate and unreasonable to whom? Can free speech be said to exist if it is constrained within a set of officially approved parameters?

O'Neill observed:

> The case revealed how degraded are the values of the Enlightenment: freedom, democracy, reason, rationalism. It also revealed that these values have not been destroyed from without by a handful of bearded men who like to shout at British soldiers—as some Islamo-obsessives would have us believe—but rather have corroded from within, being thrown off one-by-one by the fearful, increasingly illiberal institutions and ideologies of contemporary Western society.[6]

Strong stuff; but does he have a point? In pursuit of a more open and tolerant society in which people of all ethnicities and religions can feel comfortable, we are in danger of throwing away the freedom that makes all other liberties possible. Free speech must include the right to say things that most people don't like or find offensive, otherwise it is no freedom at all. We like to imagine that as civilised people we cannot abide within our midst those who are intolerant and bigoted. Yet it is quite a step from that benign intention to putting someone in prison for uttering intolerant and bigoted opinions. Yet this is what we now do.

3

Protecting Public Order

It is a great irony that, when British governments have sought to limit free speech over the past 100 years or so, they have done so in the name of democracy, liberty and tolerance. They have been confronted with a question that we still find difficult to answer; what matters most: free speech or public order? And how much of the former must we sacrifice to ensure the latter? This question has vexed our legislators for many years. Yet in addressing it they have often unwittingly, and certainly unintentionally, mimicked the despotic, the illiberal and intolerant by shutting down opinions they think most people don't want to hear.

In truth we have, by and large, been very good in this country at protecting free speech. We usually constrain it only with the heaviest heart and in what we consider to be the most extreme circumstances. But that has become less true over the years. Latterly we have been in thrall to a politically correct approach to opinions that those who make the laws simply think should not be held.

For instance, if someone wants to talk to another person about their religion, even with a view to converting them, are they not entitled to do so? Since when has proselytising been a criminal act? It is, after all, the essence of the Christian religion that its adherents seek to persuade others that it is the true way. How can it be anything other than an infringement of their liberties to say they cannot do it? You can always walk away. Yet people have been prosecuted for proselytising. This can be seen as an infringement of religious freedom; but it is in reality a restriction of free speech. The law is being used to control behaviour and the expression of an opinion.

To trace how this developed we need to go back to 1936. With Mosley's Blackshirts on the march in London's East End, a new Public Order Act criminalised behaviour that was not of itself violent but was 'threatening, abusive, insulting or disorderly' and that was intended or likely to cause a breach of the peace. The aim was to stop fascists screaming abuse at Jews in the streets; and while most civilised people wanted to shut the thugs up, there was a good deal of agonising over whether the wording was an unwarranted restriction of free speech, the beacon of liberty that marked us out from what was happening in Continental Europe at the time.

On the other hand, the fear perpetrated by the Blackshirts was itself a threat to essential British liberties. A balance had to be struck and Parliament endeavoured to do so, but not without a good deal of anguish and soul-searching. It is gratifying to think that even as Continental Europe was dragged into the gaping maw of tyranny and horror, our legislators sought to remain true to their liberal past.

The 1936 Bill was intended to prevent the sort of public order disturbances breaking out across London and other cities from getting any worse. The government, led by Stanley Baldwin, said that it would do so without impairing 'legitimate' free speech. Indeed, the people who were infringing free speech were the Blackshirts, who were turning up at public meetings to shout down ministers and close down debate. Their right to free speech was being abused to curtail the rights of others to be heard. This technique was used by the Nazis and fascist parties in Europe. Even in a country that prided itself on upholding free speech, this could hardly be tolerated. Herbert Morrison captured this in the Bill's second reading debate:

> We do not wish to pass legislation that inevitably must involve risks up to a point for all political parties and not only the political party which misbehaves itself. It is the kind of matter with which we do not want to interfere. It has, however, always been said that freedom of speech and of expression must take reasonable account of other people's freedom as well. A political organisation which has the purpose of destroying freedom of action and freedom of political organisation cannot itself very well plead the cause of freedom to do exactly as it likes. Consequently, if there be a political organisation in the State which is seeking by methods which have been successful in other countries to destroy the liberty of our people, to destroy the liberty of expression, to destroy the liberty of political organisation, of trade union organisation, and of co-operative organisation, and if that organisation is pursuing methods which are out of accord with free, liberty-loving political activity, then a State which desires to preserve liberty has a right to take action with a view to checking action which is calculated to destroy the liberty that we wish to preserve.[1]

Section 5 of the 1936 Public Order Act did not make new law so much as set down in simple terms a rule dating to 1839 that applied in the Metropolitan Police district where it was used as a measure to suppress riot and unruly behaviour. This measure was aimed at anyone 'who in any public place uses any threatening, abusive or insulting words or behaviour with intent to provoke a breach of the peace or whereby a breach of the peace may be occasioned'. Other towns and cities introduced by-laws containing identical provisions.

The Home Secretary, Sir John Simon, said at the second reading of the 1936 Public Order Bill: 'We are not seeking to enact anything startlingly new. What we are seeking to do is to provide by Act of Parliament that this shall be the law not only in London but outside.' He added: 'The general proposition in the Act seems to be perfectly fair, but while we all agree that a great deal of liberty should be allowed when political demonstrations or arguments are going on, and while it seems to me that the working of the law has been satisfactory in London, I would invite the House to lay this down as a plain and sensible proposition.'

Simon was well aware of the potential impact on free speech and devoted much of his contribution to the subject:

> Freedom of speech has been observed and has been prized in this country, perhaps, more than in any other land. We must preserve that freedom. I suggest that the law has interfered less often with the exercise of the freedom of speech than have interrupters of speech and sometimes organised interrupters at various public gatherings. There are too many people who are good speakers but bad listeners, and we must encourage people to leave freedom of utterance to those who may specially prepare for the satisfaction of others. Free speech can continue only if we observe the decencies of controversy and refrain from describing other people in outrageous terms. It is the right of the law to prevent the use of threatening abusive and insulting words likely to cause a breach of the peace. All of us engaged in public affairs have very much to endure sometimes from each other and sometimes from strangers. If we are individually injured by abuse, libel or slander, we have redress in the courts of law. In other respects we are

completely without defence. Racial abuse is perhaps the most provoking and improper of all. It arouses passions deeper than class or party criticism can, no matter how sharp that criticism may be. I hope that we shall unitedly resent these beastly and un-English attacks upon a race long resident in this country.[2]

This debate was revisited precisely 50 years later, when the Thatcher government updated public order laws in 1986 to take account of the disturbances in Brixton and Toxteth and at a succession of industrial disputes, such as the miners' strike and Wapping. Ministers also wanted to get a grip once and for all on the mayhem that had taken hold of our national sport. Every Saturday, the football terraces were a seething mass of contorted faces and vile chanting.

Opening the second reading debate on 13 January 1986, the Home Secretary Douglas Hurd, set out the case for public order as a fundamental social good that had to be balanced against the right to free speech. 'Let us not forget that the right to go about one's lawful occasions in peace is the underlying human right without which all others are nugatory,' he said. 'Quiet streets and a peaceful framework for our individual lives can never be taken for granted.'

In 1985, rioting had broken out in Brixton, spread to Birmingham and Bristol and had culminated in the murder of Pc Keith Blakelock at Broadwater Farm in Tottenham. Hurd said that while a panicky legislative response would be misguided it was 'not unreasonable' half a century on from the 1936 Act to update the law.

Much of the legislation involved modernising the language for offences such as riot and affray. It was also primarily concerned with bearing down on the scourge of football hooliganism and introduced new restrictions on marches and processions. But once again, the most controversial provision, as it had been in 1936, was Clause 5. Crucially, it removed the requirement for an intention to cause a breach of the peace. Instead, abusive or insulting behaviour was to be penalised if it was within the hearing or sight of a person 'likely to be caused harassment, alarm or distress'. In other words, the intended victim of such behaviour need not be offended; it would only require a third party to feel affronted for the provision to bite. The aim, as in 1936, was to protect vulnerable people and the general public from abuse by small groups of hooligans and racist bigots.

Hurd explained:

> The new offence is aimed at protecting those in our communities who are most vulnerable to loutish and abusive behaviour—particularly the elderly and people from the ethnic minorities... It casts a blight upon an area, whether it be a shopping precinct or a city housing estate, and makes the lives of people living there fearful and miserable. People are frightened to open their own front doors. They are kept awake by rowdy behaviour late at night. Ethnic minority families are victimised with racialist slogans and abuse. Gangs of hooligans make some pedestrian and shopping areas places where ordinary people fear to go. There cannot be many right hon. and hon. Members who do not have examples in their postbags and at their surgeries.[3]

It was never entirely clear why the 1936 law, introduced to prevent precisely the sort of behaviour identified by Hurd, needed to be reformed. Did it not suffice? Moreover, the legislation marked a departure from the original White Paper proposals in two crucial respects. There would be no requirement to prove that

actual harm, harassment or distress had been caused; and
nor would it have to be 'substantial' as originally
envisaged. Furthermore, the defendant would have to
prove that his or her conduct was reasonable. In view of
these limited safeguards against people being maliciously
accused, the maximum penalty was a £400 fine.

A legal textbook gives the following assessment of
Section 5:

> The offence under s 5 was the most controversial of the
> statutory offences in the Public Order Act 1986 both before
> and during the passage of the Bill. Whereas the repealed s 5
> of the Public Order Act 1936 (replaced by Public Order Act
> 1986, s 4) was considered the lowest-level public order
> offence prior to the 1986 Act, the offence under s 5 is more
> widely drawn and extends the criminal law into areas of
> annoyance, disturbance, and inconvenience. In particular, it
> covers behaviour which falls short of violence or the threat
> or fear of violence.[4]

The way this clause was drafted marked a significant
retreat from free speech and one for which no justification
was offered. As Gerald Kaufman, shadow home secretary
at the time, put it: 'The offence will provide no protection
for the vulnerable about whom I am primarily concerned,
but will create circumstances in which the police will
have the power to pick up anyone they choose of whose
behaviour they disapprove.'

The Times in an editorial[5] had made a similar point,
warning that the offence was extremely broad in its
potential application, and the *Daily Telegraph* said
Parliament would have to ensure tight drafting to deter
police excesses.[6] For the first time, the 1986 Act
introduced an offence of behaviour that did not require
the presence of a victim whose security was threatened.

The government agreed to amend the Bill to require the presence of a bystander, although this person did not have to be a witness and could be a police officer. In 1986, while this was a dangerous enough provision, it became far more problematic with the arrival of social media platforms not even dreamt of then. And it became even more so when additional legislation eight years later, ostensibly to deal with gypsies and a backlash against rave parties (remember them?), added intentionality to the law and increased the penalties to include prison. As we will see later, some of the most celebrated cases prosecuted under Section 5 did not involve a complaint by the intended victim of abusive language but by others who had observed it remotely on Twitter, Facebook or on TV. Ever since there have been calls for Section 5 to be modified, not least because it has been used to criminalise what many people might consider simply a point of view that others do not like.

An opportunity for reform came with the outcome of the 2010 election and the coalescence of two parties committed to rebalancing the perceived anti-liberalism of the preceding Labour government. To that end, the Coalition introduced a Freedom Bill and promised to consider the possible reform of Section 5. The campaign organisation JUSTICE said:

> Freedom of expression is arguably 'the primary right in a democracy', without which 'an effective rule of law is not possible'. In England and Wales its importance has been long recognised by the common law.[7]

In particular, JUSTICE was concerned by the way the police were interacting with members of the public who were then arrested for language used during those encounters, as almost happened to the Government chief whip Andrew Mitchell during his infamous altercation with officers at the Downing Street security gates. The official police log alleged that Mr Mitchell only ceased his alleged fulminations when he was threatened with arrest under the Public Order Act. Yet the courts have taken a dim view of the police behaving in such a thin-skinned way. In one recent case, the Court of Appeal overturned the conviction of a young suspect who repeatedly swore while being searched for drugs. The judge said police officers were so regularly on the receiving end of the 'rather commonplace' expletive used that it was unlikely to cause them 'harassment, alarm or distress'. He added that in this particular case it was 'quite impossible to infer that the group of young people who were in the vicinity were likely to have experienced alarm or distress at hearing these swear words'.

Mr Justice Bean, quoting Glidewell LJ in DPP *v* Orum (1989), noted that while it was certainly not impossible for a police officer to be the person caused 'harassment, alarm or distress' under the terms of Section 5, 'very frequently, words and behaviour with which police officers will be wearily familiar will have little emotional impact on them save that of boredom'.[8]

In other words, police officers are expected to show a degree of fortitude, and the conduct complained of in order to be criminal should go beyond that which police officers would normally come across in their duties. The Metropolitan Police Commissioner, Bernard Hogan-Howe, said that he was 'deeply disappointed' by the court ruling and his force would still arrest people who direct foul language at officers. This was the view also taken by Boris Johnson, the Mayor of London and the police authority for the capital.

If these cases get to court (and many do) they have to be considered in the light of Article 10 of the European Convention on Human Rights, which protects freedom of expression. However, this is not an unqualified right: Article 10(2) states that it may be subject to such 'restrictions or penalties as are prescribed by law and are necessary in a democratic society' in the interests of national security, for the prevention of disorder or crime or 'for the protection of the reputation or rights of others'. But the use of the offence was by no means confined to such situations. JUSTICE said:

> Our starting point is that there is no right, either in English law or in the law of the ECHR, not to be offended. While there is clearly a public interest in the criminal law protecting members of the public from being threatened or harassed by others, merely causing offence (or being likely to do so) through words or conduct in a public place should not, without more, constitute a criminal offence. Public words and conduct which some members of society would have been offended by in previous centuries (and indeed, which a minority of people with less progressive social views are probably still offended by) has been responsible for important social and political reforms: the assertion of racial and gender equality; gay Pride marches; etc. It is essential for the progress of our society that we do not now attempt to ossify public views by censoring debate on matters of current public controversy.

It added:

> Strongly held social, political and religious views mean that offence is easily taken often on both sides of a debate: for example, on topics as heterogeneous as abortion and conflict in the Middle East. Such subjects, however, remain of extreme importance and ordinary citizens, as well as the media and political classes, must be able to discuss them,

debate and demonstrate without fear of arrest and prosecution.[9]

This problem is not confined to the Public Order Act. In 2008, the Criminal Justice and Immigration Bill contained a provision against inciting hatred on the grounds of sexual orientation. For those who disapprove of the sexual conduct of other people, the risk arose that saying so would lead to arrest and prosecution.

David Waddington, the former Home Secretary, tabled an amendment in the House of Lords to protect free speech. It was resisted by the Labour government who argued that the protection of minorities from the antipathy of others outweighed the rights of the latter to express critical views that might be considered 'hateful'. The problem with this law was that it placed the police in an impossible position, required to investigate almost any complaint that an individual had expressed a negative opinion of homosexuality.

Waddington's amendment provided a protection for 'discussion or criticism of sexual conduct or practice' to the law on incitement to hatred on the grounds of sexual orientation. But the Labour government kept returning to the issue in a bid to unravel the protection inserted by Waddington. One attempt took place in July 2009 and was denounced by Lord Dear, a former chief constable and inspector of constabulary. He argued that the 'free speech' clause had helped the police. He told peers:

> Prior to this House approving the Waddington amendment a year ago, the police regularly received complaints from homosexual groups that exception was taken to remarks that homosexuality was deplored on religious grounds. They were forced to act. With the Waddington amendment the police are released from a virtual strait-jacket that was

imposed on them before. They can exercise common sense and good judgment on the day and they can police with a light touch.[10]

The Government was again defeated and the free speech protection stands, at least ostensibly, to this day. Waddington later defended his amendment from attacks, often by those who would regard themselves as on the liberal wing of politics. 'Civil liberty surely implies the freedom to express your own views, and with it a readiness to defend the right of others to express their views about you. To stir up hatred can never be right, but it would be a sad world in which every comment and criticism was assumed to have been made with evil intent.'[11]

The free speech protection echoed a similar provision inserted in an earlier measure to outlaw religious hatred, a law that the comedian Rowan Atkinson and others fought to water down for fear they would never again be able to joke about matters of faith. This protection stated that: 'Nothing in this part shall be read or given effect in a way which prohibits or restricts discussion, criticism or expressions of antipathy, dislike, ridicule, insult or abuse of particular religions or the beliefs or practices of their adherents, or of any other belief system or the beliefs or practices of its adherents, or proselytising or urging adherents of a different religion or belief system to cease practising their religion or belief system.'[12]

Labour opposed that safeguard, too, and were determined to prevent its extension to the new homophobic hate crime until they ran into opposition from peers, the Church and, once again, comedians.

Atkinson said he did not really think that he would risk prosecution for making jokes if the free speech clause

33

was repealed but dreaded 'something almost as bad—a culture of censoriousness, a questioning, negative and leaden attitude that is encouraged by legislation of this nature but is considerably and meaningfully alleviated by the free speech clause'.[13]

In a Lords debate, the Bishop of Winchester, the Right Reverend Michael Scott-Joynt, said: 'What is at stake is whether this House and this Parliament intends to outlaw, among not just Christians but others, open discussion and teaching of views that differ from the currently dominant political orthodoxy.' He said the current orthodoxy was that sexual orientation was 'more akin to ethnicity than it is to religious belief'.[14]

This hard-won protection addressed a crucial principle that has run throughout the controversies on the issue over the centuries. The aim was not to encourage abuse of others but to stop people who have no intention of stirring up hatred from being bullied and intimidated so they dare not exercise their right to free speech.

The two major pieces of public order legislation, 1936 and 1986, together with new laws of recent origin seeking to constrain hatred against others on the grounds of their religious belief or sexuality, have had a significant and deeply chilling effect on freedom of expression. The Labour government subsequently issued guidance to the police to clarify the nature of the offence of stirring up homophobic hatred. Lord Bach, a minister in the Upper House, said: 'In formulating the offence, we had no intention of stifling debate about sexual orientation or interfering with the preaching of religious doctrine, or of making it more difficult to portray homosexual characters in comedy. The question before us today is whether we need the freedom of expression provision. We have always maintained we do not. It is unnecessary but there will be those who decide to take advantage of it, to the disadvantage of others.'

But even with the protections inserted into the religious and sexual hatred laws, Section 5 of the 1986 Public Order Act has no such statutory measure of proportionality. As a result, many of the most gratuitous affronts to free speech remain cases brought under this measure: against Christians for criticising homosexuality and against two men for kissing in public; against anti-abortion, anti-capitalist and anti-Scientology protesters; against a man handing out leaflets criticising CCTV cameras and against the Oxford student arrested under Section 5 for repeatedly asking a police officer if his horse was gay.

4

Case Studies

Who said Jehovah? The case of Ben and Sharon Vogelenzang

Until the police turned up at the hotel they ran close to Liverpool's Aintree racecourse in March 2009, Ben and Sharon Vogelenzang had lived a blameless and largely anonymous life. If one thing marked them out from their fellow Merseysiders, it was their strong Christian faith. They were members of the Bootle Christian Fellowship and had owned the Bounty House hotel for some six years when a guest arrived who was to shatter their comfortable existence.

Ericka Tazi, 60, a British-born grandmother, was staying at Bounty House while having medical treatment at a local hospital. Mrs Tazi is a Muslim, a convert from Roman Catholicism, who arrived for breakfast on the last day of her stay wearing a hijab and ankle-length gown to breakfast. Most people might think her choice of garb was her own business; but for Mr and Mrs Vogelenzang, it was an affront to their beliefs. Mrs Tazi engaged them in a discussion about religion, the vehemence of which was subject to dispute but not its purport. The hoteliers were said to have called the prophet Mohammed a warlord and told Mrs Tazi she was living in bondage. She says she was subjected to a tirade of anti-Islam invective and complained to the police.

Mrs Vogelenzang told her story to a Commons committee in 2011:

Running a hotel was our dream for a long-time. We wanted to provide a place where people would feel welcome and cared-for. The business really started to take off when we contracted with the pain management centre at our local hospital to provide accommodation for people who were coming in for treatment. We received lots of referrals from 2008 onwards—and lots of nice thank you cards afterwards from the people who stayed.

One lady referred from the hospital in March 2009 was a convert to Islam. She was not the first Muslim guest we had welcomed into our hotel (which is also our home) and we have always had good relations with local people in the Muslim community. Although she had lengthy discussions with another guest about her faith, we didn't talk with her about her faith, or our own (we are Christians) until the last day of her stay. Previously she had always worn Western dress but on her final day she came to breakfast wearing a long robe. She asked if I knew she was a Muslim and I said I did. She approached me again a few minutes later to raise the subject of her Islamic dress but I was busy emptying the dishwasher.

She then initiated another conversation about her religion with my husband Ben. He tried to make light of it but the lady appeared determined to keep the conversation going. She did so by attacking the Christian faith, saying, 'Jesus was just a minor prophet and the bible is not true.' I joined the conversation saying 'we would have to disagree with you there as we are Christians.'

She referred again to the issue of Islamic dress and I said I couldn't understand why she would want to put herself into bondage. She became angry and said, 'I knew this was going to happen' and walked off.

She again raised the issue of religion with Ben and with another guest and again became angry and walked off. She left that day with the other guests, most of them exchanging the usual pleasantries and, apart from feeling a little bruised by the encounter, we didn't give it any more thought until we were told she had made a complaint to the police.[1]

At this point, common sense should have prevailed and the police should have made clear that it is not their function to intercede in an ecumenical argument between two people from different faiths. But because of the way they interpret the Public Order Act—and mindful of the climate created by hate crime laws—the police are now regularly drawn into just such arguments. It could be argued that the Vogelenzangs did not behave as hosts should, especially towards a paying guest. You would not expect to turn up for breakfast in a hotel in, say, Marrakech and be criticised for not having a beard or not covering your head. Perhaps they should have held their own counsel; after all, it is not their concern to which god others pray. The Vogelenzangs might have been intimidating; quite possibly even rude, though they deny this. But whatever the circumstances, by what stretch of the imagination and by what measure of free speech was this a matter for the criminal law?

Yet, Mrs Tazi thought her case fell within these legal parameters and so did Merseyside police, who assigned six officers from their specialist hate crime unit to investigate the Vogelenzangs. In July 2009, they were arrested and charged under Section 5 of the Public Order Act 1986 and Section 31 (1) (c) and (5) of the Crime and Disorder Act 1998—under which harassment or threat became a new kind of crime if motivated by religious or racial prejudice. Mrs Tazi, who had married a Muslim several years previously, said she had tried many other religions before turning to Islam.

'Can't people see that beneath these robes I'm just a normal English girl? I'm just Ericka, a harmless pensioner. You wouldn't look twice at me if you saw me wearing so-called Western clothes. I was a hippy once. I was also a big Beatles fan. But I've found religion. It's really important to me. I'm not extremist or anything like that. What did they [the Vogelenzangs] think, that I was a suicide bomber because of my robes?'[2]

She insisted she did not put on the hijab deliberately to provoke the hoteliers. But if she felt offended by their reaction why weren't they entitled, under the same law, to claim that their religious sensibilities had been abused? The case took months to come to court and was dismissed by Deputy District Judge Richard Clancy, after sitting through two days' evidence. But those who think that this shows the law working should consider the impact the arrest and the long wait for trial had on a perfectly innocent couple.

Mrs Vogelenzang told MPs what happened.

At the trial Ben was put on the stand first, and I saw all the stress of the previous eight months coming out as he gave his evidence. He was distraught afterwards. He sat in court crying his eyes out. The court was told my husband offended the lady by calling Mohammed a warlord. He never said that. But Hugh Tomlinson, QC, our barrister, said that even if he had, 'The fact that someone is upset or offended is not a reason for criminalising the speech used by the other person.' Thankfully, the judge reached his decision very quickly. He said the evidence against us was unreliable and implied the police should have handled matters differently and that the case should never have been brought. [3]

Yet the Crown Prosecution Service maintained it was in the public interest to have gone ahead. Sharon King, a spokesman for the CPS, said: 'We would pursue a case like this again if a similar incident was to arise in the future. It is in the public interest that incidents like this are properly investigated. We felt there was sufficient evidence in this instance to support a prosecution.'[4] In doing so, they brought threats of violence down on the heads of the couple and contributed to the collapse of their business.

Mrs Vogelenzang explained that much of their trade came from the hospital which stopped referring people to stay with them.

Since 80 per cent of our business came from them, our business collapsed. We had to sack staff and we and other family members had to work unpaid to try to keep the business afloat. We tried to persuade the hospital to refer people to us again after we were cleared. After all, the court had declared us innocent. But they wouldn't.

Our hotel business closed in September 2010 and we re-opened the premises as a social enterprise, aiming to provide respite care, a contact centre and other services for the local community. As I've said, we are Christians and we trust God to bring good out of a bad situation.

Mrs Vogelenzang summed up their ordeal thus:

Even though we were acquitted we went through a terrible ordeal which cost us our business. We lost our freedom of speech the day we were charged, because it makes you afraid to say things even though you have every right to say it.[5]

Mike Judge, a spokesman for the Christian Institute, which supported the Vogelenzangs, said: 'Important issues of religious freedom and free speech were at stake in this case. We have detected a worrying tendency in public bodies to misapply the law in a way that seems to sideline Christianity more than other faiths. People see the police standing by when Muslim demonstrators take to the streets in this country holding some pretty bloodthirsty placards, but at the same time come down hard on two Christians having a debate over breakfast.'

This is not really about Christians being treated worse than Muslims, though that does seem to be one effect of the law. It is about free speech. If the Vogelenzangs wanted to dispute with Mrs Tazi about the merits of their respective religions that should not be a matter for the criminal law. As their solicitor, David Whiting, said: 'They have every right to defend their religious beliefs and explain those beliefs to others who do not hold similar views.'

But while the courts upheld that right in their case, the law as currently framed encourages the police to intercede in matters of behaviour and the expression of opinion that they have no business getting involved in. Moreover, the Vogelenzangs had months of worry and lost their business as a result of the publicity.

A law introduced to stop disorder on the streets has become a means of controlling opinions that are considered unacceptable, without any obvious reason why they should be apart from the fact that someone else might not like them.

Neil Addison, a prominent criminal barrister and expert in religious law, said: 'The purpose of the Public Order Act is to prevent disorder, but I'm very concerned that the police are using it merely because someone is offended. It should be used where there is violence, yobbish behaviour or gratuitous personal abuse. It should never be used where there has been a personal conversation or debate with views firmly expressed.

'If someone is in a discussion and they don't like what they are hearing, they can walk away.'[6]

Who are you calling a cult?

It is one thing for the police to intervene when there is a difference of opinion between individuals. But it is quite another to seek to prosecute someone for stating

41

something that most people accept as true. Scientology, a set of beliefs created by L. Ron Hubbard in 1952 that espouses the idea that humans are descended from an exiled race of aliens called Thetans, has often and widely been called a cult. In fact, a 1984 court ruling described it as a cult. Yet when a 15-year-old boy demonstrated outside the church's headquarters in the City of London bearing a placard to that effect, he was served with a court summons under the Public Order Act as amended by the 1998 Criminal Justice Act. City of London police said he had refused to put down a placard saying 'Scientology is not a religion, it is a dangerous cult' during a peaceful protest. A file was passed to the Crown Prosecution Service, which ruled the wording was neither 'abusive nor insulting' to the church and no further action would be taken against the boy.

'Our advice is that it is not abusive or insulting and there is no offensiveness, as opposed to criticism, neither in the idea expressed nor in the mode of expression. No action will be taken against the individual.'[7] But even if it had been insulting, so what? Scientologists undoubtedly regard being described as a cult insulting; but it should be perfectly within anyone's rights to call it whatever they want. The teenager's mother said the decision was 'a victory for free speech.' But only as far is it went: a summons should never have been issued in the first place and is another example of the chilling effect of the last government's so-called 'hate' laws that the police even considered it appropriate. James Welch of the campaign group Liberty said: 'Democracy is all about clashing ideas and the police should protect peaceful protest, not stifle it.'

Seal of Approval

Over-zealous policing of free expression has not been confined to religion. In 2006 in Evesham, eight animal rights campaigners were issued with orders under the Public Order Act requiring them to remove from public sight toy seals covered in red dye as part of their protest against the annual culling of cubs in Canada. Police said the action was taken to prevent 'disorder, or distress or disruption'.

Lynn Sawyer, one of the organisers from Evesham, said: 'I don't see how people could be offended by cuddly toys. We were just in the street, we were not outside a fur shop or anything like that.' A West Mercia police spokesman said: 'The order was issued to prevent disorder, or distress or disruption to passers-by. These orders are used where the senior officer policing any event or incident considers that it could give rise to serious disorder, disruption to the community, or intimidation, or could cause harassment or distress.'[8]

Just a few weeks earlier, police in Herefordshire seized three golly toys in Bromyard, under race-hate laws. They raided the Pettifers hardware and gift store in the High Street after a visitor to the town complained about the dolls. There were demonstrations in support of the shopkeeper, Donald Reynolds, somewhat light-heartedly demanding the release of the 'Bromyard Three'—the dolls. But the Crown Prosecution Service got the message and decided not to pursue charges. Mr Reynolds said: 'Everyone seems to agree that there is nothing racist about the dolls. They are just very popular and people like to see them back.' Herefordshire Police returned the golliwogs to Mr Reynolds—with a letter advising him about the sensitivity surrounding the controversial dolls.[9]

Barking Mad

When Newcastle teenager Kyle Little growled and barked at two Labradors in April 2007, the dogs' owner thought he was just being 'a daft young lad'. But two police officers who witnessed the incident arrested the 19-year-old for committing a public order offence. Little, who had earlier been warned by the officers for using bad language, was charged and convicted at magistrates court of causing harassment, alarm or distress. He was fined £50 and ordered to pay £150 costs. However, the case went to appeal before Judge Beatrice Bolton at Newcastle Crown Court who was less impressed than the magistrates with the case. She said: 'I'm sure an expert on Labradors could no doubt explain how distressed the dogs were, but I don't think Section 5 of the Public Order Act applies to dogs.' She added: 'Growling or barking at a dog does not amount to a Section 5 offence, even if a defendant has been told by the police to curb his language.'[10] The judge quashed the conviction and rebuked the prosecuting authorities, saying: 'The law is not an ass.' The cost to the taxpayer: £8,000.

Little, from Newcastle, said outside court that he had seen the dogs leaping up on railings. 'They were both barking their heads off and so I did a daft little growl and went woof woof at them. The next thing I knew, I had been grabbed by the two police officers who bent my arms up behind my back and handcuffed me. They threw me into a van and whisked me off to the police station where they threw me into a cell for about five hours.' Dog owner Sunita Vedhara said: 'He was messing about being a daft young lad. We didn't want to see him prosecuted, but the police came and said he was being taken to court, which we found surprising. The dogs weren't really upset by it at all.'[11]

Is your police horse gay?

The most notorious example of the police responding to the politically inspired climate against 'hate' came with the arrest of Oxford student Sam Brown in 2005. The Balliol undergraduate was on a night out in the city celebrating the end of his finals in English when he approached two mounted policemen. Brown asked one of the officers if he knew his horse was gay and was arrested. He was taken handcuffed to a police station where he was given a fixed penalty notice under the Public Order Act after spending the night in a cell. The Crown Prosecution Service a few months later wisely decided not to pursue the case but once again an arrest had been made and an individual's life seriously discomfited at the prospect of a criminal conviction. But were the police contrite? Not a bit of it. A spokesman for Thames Valley Police said: 'He made homophobic comments that were deemed offensive to people passing by.'[12]

Preaching to the converted

Street preachers are the sort of people most of us would cross the road to avoid; but public evangelism has been around for thousands of years, albeit often at great risk to the proselytisers. Doomsayers bearing placards warning the end is nigh or denouncing sinners have been a fairly constant fixture in our towns and cities for many years. But increasingly they have to be careful what it is they oppose. Harry Hammond, an elderly preacher, was in Bournemouth's main square on 13 October 2001, taking part in a demonstration. He held up a large double-sided sign bearing the words 'Jesus Gives Peace, Jesus is Alive, Stop Immorality, Stop Homosexuality, Stop Lesbianism, Jesus is Lord'.

When some passers-by became angry and tried to remove the sign, two police officers arrived and arrested Hammond, charging him under Section 5 of the Public Order Act 1986. No one in the crowd was charged. In the past it is at least debatable that the police would have felt it their duty to protect Mr Hammond from the threats of violence from the crowd rather than to arrest him; but the climate has been ineradicably altered by the whole concept of 'hate crime' which was very much in the news in 2001 after the Stephen Lawrence inquiry.

In April 2002, Bournemouth magistrates fined Hammond £300 and ordered him to pay costs of £395. The court ordered the destruction of the placards. Shortly after his trial, Hammond died. In 2004 campaigners tried to launch a posthumous appeal but failed. The judges ruled that that Hammond's behaviour 'went beyond legitimate protest' and that Hammond's right to freedom of expression under Section 10 of the European Convention on Human Rights was constrained by a legitimate concern to prevent disorder and that there was a pressing social need for the restriction. Peter Tatchell, the gay rights campaigner, offered to testify on Hammond's behalf at the appeal, calling the case 'an outrageous assault on civil liberties'.[13]

Dale Mcalpine also fell foul of this officially-inspired atmosphere of disapproval of views considered to be beyond the pale. A 42-year-old energy industry worker, he was arrested in April 2010 while delivering open-air sermons in his home town of Workington, in Cumbria. A committed Christian, Mr Mcalpine is a weekend street evangelist of the sort that most people probably cross the road to avoid but who is entitled to express his views, which he did alongside two friends in a shopping precinct in Workington's town centre as he had done for five years. Mr Mcalpine also told the Commons committee looking into the Protection of Freedom Bill what happened to him.[14]

On Tuesday 20th April I went with two friends into Workington Town Centre where we set up to preach in Campbell Savours Way. While one of the other men was preaching I saw two Police Community Support Officers walk up and stop outside a nearby shop. They were discussing what my friend was saying. A town centre official joined their discussion.

I then had a discussion with the town centre official who told me that our preaching was wrong and tried to convince me that the Bible was not clear and had more grey areas than what I was presenting. We had a short discussion where I explained to her that Jesus said unless we forsake our sins we will perish, she said I was talking 'nonsense' and called me arrogant, she had to leave but said she would return and looked forward to continuing our conversation.

As the woman left, one of the two officers, PCSO Sam Adams, approached her and had a brief chat before walking towards him. Mr Adams said there had been complaints and warned him that if he made racist or homophobic remarks he could be arrested.

I said I was not racist or homophobic. It was quite intimidating to be accused of that by a man in a uniform and threatened with arrest. I explained that I preach what the bible teaches about sin. The bible says we are all sinners and describes many different sins. Homosexual activity is just one of them. The gospel is about how we can be forgiven by God and that is only through Jesus Christ. It is impossible to talk about forgiveness without talking about sin. It would be like trying to talk about medicine without talking about what symptoms the medicine cures.

The PCSO said 'I am offended. I am a homosexual.' He told me he was the LGBT liaison officer. I replied that homosexuality was still a sin. He left. I discussed what had happened with my colleague and we agreed that we would not mention homosexuality in our preaching. (We had not planned to anyway.) I got up on to my little step-ladder and preached about evolution and that God is our creator also about the need to repent of sin and forgiveness through Jesus Christ, I mentioned sins like adultery, blasphemy and drunkenness, I did not mention homosexuality.

After a while, PCSO Adams returned and was joined by three uniformed constables.

I was now surrounded by five men in uniforms. The opening question from one officer was 'What have you been saying homophobic-wise?' I said homophobia was hatred of homosexuals and I do not hate homosexuals. I said the only time I had said anything about homosexuality was to the PCSO and only then after he had raised the subject with me. I said anyway it was not against the law to say that homosexuality is a sin and referred to the recent vote in Parliament to include a free speech clause in a new homophobic incitement offence.

The officer replied, 'It is against the law. Listen mate, we're pretty sure. You're under arrest for a racially aggravated Section 5 offence.' Not only was I shocked beyond belief at being arrested (I have never been arrested in my life) but I was bewildered that he was talking about racial aggravation. I hadn't said a word about race.

He read me my rights and I was led away by the arm to a police van. I was taken to the police station and held in a cell to wait to be interviewed. I had my finger prints and DNA taken and they checked on me every hour. From my arrest to my release I was detained for 7 hours and 46 minutes. I was charged with using 'threatening, abusive or insulting' words 'to cause harassment, alarm or distress', contrary to Section 5 of the Public Order Act.

As part of his bail conditions, Mr Mcalpine was told he must not preach in public until after his trial, an extraordinary restriction of his liberties and one that suggests the problem was his preaching and not the content. Like many others in his position, he also felt compelled to insist that he was not homophobic ('some of my best friends are gay') but this is beside the point. It should not matter whether he has gay friends or whether he disdains the lifestyle of homosexuals or anyone else.

Mr Mcalpine appeared before Workington magistrates but the Crown Prosecution Service said they were discontinuing the case due to lack of evidence. Lawyers acting for Mr Mcalpine gave notice of a civil action against Cumbria police, which paid him £7,000 plus costs in an out-of-court settlement.

Needless to say, I was not concerned about compensation but about freedom of speech. I hope I practice what I preach when I talk about forgiveness. I forgive the officers who arrested me. But if no-one stands up when the police start arresting people for no good reason, we are all in trouble. The fact that the police admitted liability proves that the way they used Section 5 to arrest and charge me was wrong. But I still think the law should be changed to stop the same thing happening again. It is too easy for someone to claim to be offended and summon the police to arrest the person who offended them under Section 5. In my case, their own LGBT liaison officer appears to have called them in to arrest me. Perhaps they felt they could not say no.

Mr Mcalpine continued:

People might not agree with my views about sin and forgiveness. But everyone has views that are offensive to someone. Section 5 seems to be so all-encompassing that it can be used to arrest people just for expressing controversial opinions. Today it is views about morals. Tomorrow it could be views about foreign policy or climate-change or budget-cuts.[15]

Mr Mcalpine's views may not find favour with many people; others might agree with him. It is not for the police to decide which side of the argument is right. But the hate crime laws introduced by the Labour government sent a signal, whether subliminal or direct, to the police that they should consider disapproving comments about someone's sexuality to be potentially unlawful.

Surely, legislation that permits the arrest of a Christian preacher in an English town for quoting from the Bible needs to be repealed.

5

What Happened to Common Law Protections?

The odd thing about the pursuit and arrest of preachers like Mr Mcalpine or Harry Hammond is that jurisprudence on what can be said within the law without constituting a breach of the peace was set down by the High Court in 1999. The case concerned a Christian evangelist, Alison Redmond-Bate, who on 2 October 1997 was preaching with two friends outside Wakefield Cathedral in Yorkshire. The police received complaints about them and an officer warned the women not to interrupt people walking by. They ignored him, and after 20 minutes, a crowd of more than a hundred people had gathered (most of whom showed hostility towards the three women). When they refused to stop preaching after further requests from the police, they were arrested. Redmond-Bate was later convicted at Wakefield Magistrates Court and charged with 'obstructing a police officer in the execution of his duty'.

The appeal to the High Court asked the judges to consider whether it was reasonable for the police officer to arrest the appellant who had not conducted herself in a manner which would be said to constitute an offence under the Public Order Act 1986.

Mr Justice Sedley in his ruling stated:

> I am unable to see any lawful basis for the arrest or therefore the conviction... There was no suggestion of highway obstruction. Nobody had to stop and listen. If they did so,

they were as free to express the view that the preachers should be locked up or silenced as the appellant and her companions were to preach.[1]

He said that free speech included not only the inoffensive, but the irritating, the contentious, the eccentric, the heretical, the unwelcome and the provocative, provided it did not tend to provoke violence. Sedley took the view that the Crown Court, in dismissing Redmond-Bate's appeal, had acted illiberally and illogically and Redmond-Bate had been preaching about morality, God and the Bible, which were regularly the topic of church sermons and religious broadcasts.

Astonishingly, Redmond-Bate was one of many victims of a police crackdown on street evangelism that was happening in the late 1990s. Malcolm Nowell, a Halifax solicitor who represented many of the preachers, said many of the Faith Ministry had been wrongly held in custody, some for as long as three weeks. The case, said Nowell, at the time upheld the freedom to express lawful matters in a way which other people might take great exception to.[2] But the key point there is 'lawful matters'. When so-called hate crime laws were introduced, police no longer regarded a preacher saying that, for instance, homosexuality is a sin as expressing a lawful opinion.

We have, in other words, moved beyond the right to say something offensive provided it does not cause violence, as Lord Justice Sedley put it (which is how free speech had long been understood), to say only contentious things that have been officially approved for utterance. Sedley's summing up was a masterful exposition of a concept of free speech that no longer exists. 'Freedom only to speak inoffensively is not worth having,' he said.

What Speakers' Corner (where the law applies as fully as anywhere else) demonstrates is the tolerance which is both extended by the law to opinion of every kind and expected by the law in the conduct of those who disagree, even strongly, with what they hear.

From the condemnation of Socrates to the persecution of modern writers and journalists, our world has seen too many examples of state control of unofficial ideas. A central purpose of the European Convention on Human Rights has been to set close limits to any such assumed power. We in this country continue to owe a debt to the jury which in 1670 refused to convict the Quakers William Penn and William Mead for preaching ideas which offended against state orthodoxy.[3]

Yet ten years later, Dale Mcalpine found himself pretty much in the same position as Alison Redmond-Brown and despite the ruling of the High Court.

After the Hammond case, the Association of Chief Police Officers updated its national guidance document, *Keeping The Peace*, to remind officers that they must be aware that the right to free speech allows people to express unpopular views as long as 'their conduct is reasonable or the actual or potential violence provoked in others is "wholly unreasonable"'. The guidance also makes clear that though officers themselves may be victims of 'harassment, alarm or distress', they are expected to have thicker skins than the public, and they have a responsibility to protect the rights of the speaker.

What is interesting about this document is that it takes as its starting point not English common law protections for freedom of speech but the European Convention on Human Rights Article 11, which enshrines freedom of association and assembly. As the document states, there is 'no legal basis in domestic law for describing a public protest as inherently unlawful' though there is a common law offence of breach of the peace which is committed when an individual causes harm or is likely to cause harm to another or puts a person in fear that harm will be done or violence caused. In deciding whether a breach of the peace has occurred, the police must be mindful of the rights to free expression and 'act proportionately'. But how are they to make that judgment, especially in a climate where they are constantly being bombarded from the training room onwards with a set of values to which people are expected to subscribe?

Imagine how much more difficult it is for police officers when they are reminded of Articles 9 and 10 of the ECHR which enshrine the rights to freedom of belief and expression. 'This applies not only to information, ideas or opinions that are popular or fashionable or regarded as inoffensive of a matter of indifference but also to those that offend, shock or disturb... Expressions of racist opinions or ideas, statements which incite violence and hate speech are not permitted by the (ECHR).'[4] The guidance contradicts itself in the space of a paragraph: you can say what you want provided what you say does not constitute 'racist opinions' or 'hate speech'. And who is to decide that?

The guidance states that officers need to distinguish 'between the message or opinions being communicated and the manner in which it is conveyed. It is the conduct or behaviour which is gratuitous or calculated to insult that is the subject of the offence rather than the public expression of an offensive message or speech.'[5]

But how does that square with the earlier guidance just a few paragraphs earlier that 'hate speech' has no protection? How is the 'public expression of an offensive message or speech' to be differentiated from 'hate speech'? Furthermore, at what point does an opinion amount to 'stirring up' hatred by others against people on the grounds of their race, religion or sexuality?

It is hardly surprising that in this confusing *mélange* of different rights, liberties and statute laws, the police often feel they are caught in the middle and unjustly called upon to act as arbiters of political correctness.

The obvious problem is the subjective nature of an insult. While most of us can recognise abusive language when we hear it, in what way is it a crime to take issue with someone else's opinion, or even their religion? This is likely to become more problematic as the gay marriage debate continues to provoke controversy, because Christian groups are worried that they will fall foul of these various laws for expressing opposition to the idea. It will be one thing to challenge the political basis of the proposed legislation but what happens when that strays into adopting a strongly moral position that someone else finds hurtful?

In a civilised country, people should not be abusive or gratuitously offensive to each other; but should being boorish or foul-mouthed be a crime as opposed to a social misdemeanour?

Section 5 of the Public Order Act was devised predominantly to stop crowds of louts, usually football fans, swearing at one another. Of course, this was the purpose behind the 1986 Act: clearly tribal supporters hurling abuse at one another do not themselves feel harassed or insulted, but innocent bystanders, especially families with children, assuredly will.

The problem is that a law introduced for one purpose is now turning into an instrument of thought engineering.

The Conservative MP Dominic Raab unearthed 18,000 uses of Section 5 in 2009 alone.[6] It turns out that the police use it a lot to keep control of protests which are, almost by definition, often directed at an unsympathetic audience and designed to cause offence.

Mike Harris of the Index on Censorship said:

> Finding the correct balance between public order and legitimate protest isn't always easy. But asking the police to patrol offence has undermined public trust in them. Rightly so, for it is not the job of local bobbies or magistrates to protect citizens from insult. Christian preachers or mouthy anarchists may irritate, but in an open, free society, robust opinion will insult you: perhaps we all just need to get used to it.[7]

But does it matter if so many of these patently absurd cases get thrown out? Simon Calvert, the Campaign Director of Reform Section 5, thinks it does.

> Many of the more absurd cases which make the news do end in acquittal, often when a civil liberties group gets involved, and I have heard defenders of Section 5 claim that the high acquittal rate demonstrates that the law is working. This is palpable nonsense. A law should not be judged a success on the basis of the number of people proved innocent of having broken it. Such a law should not exist in the first place.[8]

Another difficulty is where police efforts to deal with disorder, following the efforts of successive governments to crack down on anti-social behaviour, become entangled with free speech.

Lord Justice Sedley in his 1999 judgment drew a distinction between expression that someone might find hurtful and language likely to incite violence or physical harm to others. In simple terms, it is the old adage that sticks and stones may break my bones but names will never hurt me.

The Crown Prosecution Service's latest guidelines for the Section 5 offence says:

> Whether behaviour can be properly categorised as disorderly is a question of fact. Disorderly behaviour does not require any element of violence, actual or threatened; and it includes conduct that is not necessarily threatening, abusive or insulting. It is not necessary to prove any feeling of insecurity, in an apprehensive sense, on the part of a member of the public (*Chambers and Edwards v DPP* [1995] Crim LR 896).
>
> ...There must be a person within the sight or hearing of the suspect who is likely to be caused harassment, alarm or distress by the conduct in question. A police officer may be such a person, but remember that this is a question of fact to be decided in each case by the magistrates. In determining this, the magistrates may take into account the familiarity which police officers have with the words and conduct typically seen in incidents of disorderly conduct (*DPP v Orum* [1988] Crim L R 848).
>
> Although the existence of a person who is caused harassment alarm and distress must be proved, there is no requirement that they actually give evidence. In appropriate cases, the offence may be proved on a police officer's evidence alone.
>
> Police officers are aware of the difficult balance to be struck in dealing with those whose behaviour may be perceived by some as exuberant high spirits but by others as disorderly. In such cases, informal methods of disposal may be appropriate and effective; but if this approach fails and the disorderly conduct continues then criminal proceedings may be necessary.

In deciding whether a charge under Section 5 is appropriate, the nature of the conduct must be considered in light of the penalty that the suspect is likely to receive on conviction...

...By virtue of section 31(1)(c)of the Crime and Disorder Act 1998 (as amended by the Anti-Terrorism, Crime and Security Act 2001), Section 5 is capable of being charged as a discrete racially or religiously aggravated offence.[9]

In a report in 2009, the Joint Committee on Human Rights tackled this issue in the context of policing public protest:

We recommend that the Government amend Section 5 of the Public Order Act 1986 so that it cannot be used inappropriately to suppress the right to free speech, by deleting the reference to language or behaviour that is merely 'insulting'. This amendment would provide proportionate protection to individuals' right to free speech, whilst continuing to protect people from threatening or abusive speech. We suggest such an amendment.

Campaigners had hoped that the Protection of Freedoms Bill would bring about reform of Section 5, but when the legislation was published in 2011 no change was proposed.

A campaign, Feel Free to Insult Me, kept the argument on the boil and finally, in December 2012, the matter was debated and put to a vote in the House of Lords. An amendment moved by Lord Dear, a former chief constable for the West Midlands force, removed the word 'insulting' from Section 5 of the 1986 Act.

'The amendment seeks to curb what I believe is an increasing misuse of the criminal law so as to curb or prevent the proper exercise of free speech,' Lord Dear said. 'With the wisdom of hindsight, it is clear that there has been a steady increase of cases where the words "insulting words or behaviour causing distress" were being misapplied in circumstances where individuals or organisations disagreed with comments made about their own sexual orientation, general beliefs or objectives, and where the criminal sanction offered by Section 5 was used by them deliberately to curb or suppress the proper exercise of free speech, either by prosecution, or by utilising the undoubted chilling effect of a threat of prosecution.'[10]

Lord Dear accepted that the police were partly to blame for failing always to exercise the 'degree of common sense and discretion that would properly have resulted in a blind eye being turned to the conduct in question'. He added: 'Often, however, the police have been manipulated by those whose tactic has been to complain to the police on the spot and insist on police intervention, with the express or implied threat of a complaint against them unless action is taken. A now often risk-averse police service, and sometimes risk-averse prosecutors as well, have found it safer to mount a prosecution and leave the courts to adjudicate.'

Lord Dear said that he had hardly heard an argument in favour of retaining the word 'insulting' in Section 5 despite his high-profile association with the campaign for its repeal. However, there were powerful opponents, among them the Police Federation and the Crown Prosecution Service. Yet the CPS, Lord Dear reported, had been unable to identify a case in which the alleged behaviour leading to a conviction could not properly have been characterised as 'abusive' as well as 'insulting'.

Lord Dear considered this to be 'a very significant message indeed'; yet it suggests that the very same people whose arrest and prosecution he had sought to prevent by amending the law would still be criminalised by another definition in the same Act. If free speech is infringed by stopping an individual insulting another, does the same not apply if they 'abuse' them? What's the difference? The agreement of the Lords to Dear's amendment was hailed as a great victory for free speech but it might just be a hollow one if Christian preachers, for instance, are simply pursued for abuse rather than insult. After all, if someone says they find gay marriage repellent is that abuse or an insult?

If anything, Lord Dear's argument was too narrowly defined. As he acknowledged, Section 5 in its curtailed form would still allow prosecution for 'threatening or abusive behaviour', and there were, he pointed out, tougher and more targeted laws, such as incitement to racial hatred, and a range of aggravated offences where hostility to the group to which the individual belongs is taken into account.

'Along with general laws, such as public nuisance and breach of the peace, these give the police all the powers they need to protect minority groups,' said Lord Dear. Be that as it may; but this was supposed to be about protecting free speech.

The Home Office Minister, Lord Taylor of Holbeach, disputed that this was a free speech matter at all since Section 5 does not make it an offence for one person simply to insult, abuse or even threaten another. 'For the offence to be committed the words or behaviour used, or the insulting writing or picture displayed, must be within the sight or hearing of a person likely to be caused harassment, alarm or distress,' he said.

'It is perfectly possible for a person lawfully to express views in public, which are considered by others to be insulting, abusive or threatening without being likely to cause harassment, alarm or distress, and therefore not to contravene Section 5.' Perhaps so; but they will almost certainly contravene the plethora of 'hate crimes'.

This confusion has never been cleared up by the courts. In Percy v DPP, the High Court ruled that for conduct to constitute a breach of the peace, it must involve violence or the threat of violence. The violence need not be perpetrated by the defendant, provided that the natural consequence of his conduct, was that others would be provoked to violence.[11] However as we have already seen in Redmane-Bate v DPP, lawful behaviour, even if provocative, may not be sufficient to constitute a breach of the peace.[12]

This is a question of balance and there are strong indications that we have got it wrong. As was pointed out earlier, the way Section 5 of the 1986 Act was framed was fundamentally different from previous laws, including those in the predecessor 1936 Act. Legal academics observed at the time that: 'it is more widely drawn and extends the criminal law into areas of annoyance, disturbance, and inconvenience. In particular, it covers behaviour which falls short of violence or the threat or fear of violence.'[13] So the Government's assertion that it is simply upholding a long established principle, balancing free speech with the rights of people not to be intimidated or abused, is simply not true.

The only consistent argument in this debate has been advanced by the campaign group Liberty which has called for the repeal of Section 5 in its entirety and a complete review of public order offences. That would still leave Section 4 of the 1986 Act on the Statute Book. This outlaws threatening, abusive or insulting words or behaviour with intent to cause a person to believe that immediate unlawful violence will be used against him. Section 4A was added by the 1994 Criminal Justice and Public Order Act. Under this, a person is guilty of an offence if, with intent to cause a person harassment, alarm or distress, he (a) uses threatening, abusive or insulting words or behaviour, or disorderly behaviour, or (b) displays any writing, sign or other visible representation which is threatening, abusive or insulting, thereby causing that or another person harassment, alarm or distress.

In other words, Section 4 requires a credible threat of violence and 4A requires intention. Section 5 is not needed at all and should be repealed.

As observed earlier, when the Racial and Religious Hatred Act was going through Parliament, a freedom of speech protection was inserted stating that:

> Nothing in this Part shall be read or given effect in a way which prohibits or restricts discussion, criticism or expressions of antipathy, dislike, ridicule, insult or abuse of particular religions or the beliefs or practices of their adherents, or of any other belief system or the beliefs or practices of its adherents, or proselytising or urging adherents of a different religion or belief system to cease practising their religion or belief system.

Since this is Parliament's most recent expression on the issue of free speech, it is an abuse of power for the police to continue to use Section 5 of the Public Order Act to override it.

6

Free Speech in the Age of Twitter and YouTube

When Paul Chambers, then 26, discovered that his flight to Belfast from Robin Hood Airport had been cancelled because of snow in January 2010, he was angry and frustrated. With his plans to spend the weekend with his girlfriend disrupted, he gave vent to his annoyance to his 600 followers on Twitter. 'Crap! Robin Hood airport is closed. You've got a week and a bit to get your shit together otherwise I am blowing the airport sky high!!' A week later, an off-duty manager at the airport found the message while carrying out an unrelated computer search, and although the message was not considered credible as a threat, the management contacted the police anyway. What was obviously a joke—and one in his own name, too—was treated as akin to a terrorist threat.

'When I was arrested on 13 January at work by four police officers, it came as a bit of a shock,' said Chambers.[1] 'Call me naive or ignorant, but the heightened state of panic over terror issues was not something I considered as relating to me in any way – until I was arrested, shoved into a police car in front of colleagues, hauled off to Doncaster police station, and interviewed for the rest of the day. My iPhone, laptop and desktop hard drive were confiscated during a search of my house. It was terrifying and humiliating.'

Chambers imagined the lunacy would end at this point but a month later he was charged with 'sending a public electronic message that was grossly offensive or of an indecent, obscene or menacing character contrary to the Communications Act 2003'. 'This first appeared to be an absolute offence, much the same as speeding: conviction does not depend on *mens rea*. For a stupid mistake, I was faced with the prospect of a career-ruining criminal conviction. After fresh legal advice it turned out I could argue I had no intention and awareness to commit the crime, and I could plead not guilty. Even after all the preceding absurdity and near-breakdown-inducing stress, I was confident common sense would prevail in my day in court.'

That was not to be. In May 2010, Chambers appeared before magistrates in Doncaster where he was fined £385 and ordered to pay £600 costs. He lost his job with a car parts company as a result.

After the hearing he said: 'Whatever happens now, I remain terrified. Terrified of speaking my mind, terrified that my life has potentially been ruined. Most of the authorities could see it for what it was, and yet I find myself with a conviction because the Crown Prosecution Service decided it was in the public interest to prosecute. It would appear we live in such a hyper-sensitive world that we cannot engage in hyperbole, however misguided, without having civil liberties trampled on by, at best, heavy-handed police. I would have fully accepted the police coming to my house to question me; it would have taken all of five minutes to realise what had happened. I would have learned my lesson and no taxpayer money would have been wasted on a frivolous prosecution. I have had some very dark days, and my family has been put through the wringer, because I made one silly joke.'[2]

Is this a free speech case or just a case of ludicrous over-reaction? Was Chambers's right to make a joke and to have it treated accordingly being challenged here or is there a legitimate national security issue at stake? After all, the untrammelled right falsely to shout 'fire' in a crowded theatre has never been acknowledged and indeed, this example was used by Oliver Wendell Holmes in the 1919 American supreme court judgment *Schenck v. United States* as a justification for restricting free expression consistent with the terms of the First Amendment of the United States Constitution.

Holmes's example remains the benchmark by which to measure when the guarantees of free speech can be set aside because the speaker has behaved in a reckless or malicious fashion. Yet this is a dangerous precedent. As the late writer and polemicist Christopher Hitchens said:

> Everyone knows the fatuous verdict of the greatly over-praised Justice Oliver Wendell Holmes, who, when asked for an actual example of when it would be proper to limit speech or define it as an action, gave that of shouting 'fire' in a crowded theatre. It's very often forgotten what he was doing in that case was sending to prison a group of Yiddish-speaking socialists, whose literature was printed in a language most Americans couldn't read, opposing Mr Wilson's participation in the First World War, and the dragging of the United States into that sanguinary conflict, which the Yiddish-speaking socialists had fled from Russia to escape. In fact it could be just as plausibly argued that the Yiddish-speaking socialists who were jailed by the excellent and greatly over-praised Judge Oliver Wendell Holmes were the real fire-fighters, were the ones shouting fire when there really was a fire in a very crowded theatre indeed. And who is to decide?[3]

Who indeed? Moreover, in the case of a well-known individual, is the law applied differently? When the diver Tom Daley failed to win a medal in the Olympic synchronised event, he received a message via Twitter that was hurtful and intended to be so. Daley, whose father had died the previous year from cancer, was sent an anonymous tweet that read: 'You let your dad down I hope you know that.' This was followed up with: 'Hope your [sic] crying now you should be why can't you ever produce for your country your [sic] just a diver anyway a over-hyped p****.'

Daley himself re-tweeted the message to his 900,000 followers with the comment 'after giving it my all, you get idiots sending me this...' The resulting public anger prompted the police to intervene and they quickly identified the sender of the tweet as Reece Messer, a teenager from Weymouth who appeared to be in the habit of sending similarly obnoxious messages to all and sundry. Officers from Dorset police arrested Messer at a bedsit in the seaside town on suspicion of sending a malicious communication. Questioned for several hours, he was eventually released with a formal warning for harassment. The question that arises is whether this was something the police should have been involved in at all. Certainly, the comments were offensive and clearly upset Daley; but is that sufficient to lead to someone's arrest? If Daley had been black or Muslim, the consequences for Messer would likely have been worse since racial or religious aggravation could have been a factor.

The atmosphere that these laws engender leads to disproportionate and unjust penalties. When the foot-baller Fabrice Muamba collapsed while playing for Bolton in a match being televised live, Liam Stacey, a 21-year-old university student, also took to Twitter with the words: 'LOL [laughing out loud], **** Muamba. He's dead!!! #haha.' He responded to criticism of that message with vile racist tweets.

As a result of what was evidently an unpleasant outburst by a stupid young man who was watching the match in a pub and had had too much to drink, Stacey's life has been turned upside down. He was thrown off his biology course at Swansea University and then sentenced to 56 days in jail. Stacey's messages provoked public revulsion, especially as Muamba's televised collapse appeared to have inspired a mood of near hysteria, with days of medical bulletins being broadcast on the main news even though he made a full recovery. Stacey's reaction would be considered appalling by most people; but how is the punishment appropriate? District judge John Charles sent him to prison to 'reflect public outrage' at his outburst. He told Stacey: 'Not just the footballer's family, not just the footballing world, but the whole world were literally praying for Muamba's life. Your comments aggravated this situation.'[4] The whole world? Have we gone mad? The answer to that question is quite possibly yes in view of what happened to Stacey.

He told BBC Wales after his release from jail: 'What I struggle to get my head around was the week or two before I was just a normal kid getting on with my work in university, getting on with life, playing rugby with all my mates, then a week or two later I was just going to prison, everything had been turned upside down,' he said. He was, at least, to be given the opportunity to sit his final exams as an external candidate.

But hardly anyone has expressed astonishment that we have jailed someone for voicing a set of opinions, however nasty they may be, which did not in any way threaten anyone else or seek to inspire violence. The individual against whom they were initially aimed was not even the complainant. Essentially, the law is being used to shut down views that do not conform to what a majority wishes to consider proper.

John Kampfner, an external adviser to Google on free expression, writing in the *Guardian*, said: 'The authorities are not solely to blame for this state of affairs. We the public, both Twitter-using and non-Twitter-using, have elevated taking offence to a human right. We see hurt and danger around every corner and lurking in every missive. For sure, some are beyond the pale. One or two might be prosecutable. But, for the most part we should develop a thicker skin, keep calm and carry on.'[5]

In the Chambers appeal at the High Court, the Lord Chief Justice Lord Judge and his colleagues tried to provide a definition of Twitter: '"Tweets" include expressions of opinion, assertions of fact, gossip, jokes (bad ones as well as good ones), descriptions of what the user is or has been doing, or where he has been, or intends to go. Effectively it may communicate any information at all that the user wishes to send, and for some users, at any rate, it represents no more and no less than conversation without speech.' And in a conversation, people can say offensive things without being arrested and jailed. Surely it is possible for the police and courts to distinguish between direct incitement to violence and drunken ramblings, whether or not they are racist or homophobic. The court should also stop Section 127 of the Communications Act 2003, which predates Twitter, being used as a catch-all for online behaviour that isn't caught by other laws. This is a misuse of the statute for which it was never intended.

Nor is this culture confined to the law. When the blogger Alexander Boot placed an article on the *Mail Online* website in which he stated that he regarded homosexuality to be 'a departure from the norm', a campaign was mounted to get a complaint to the Press Complaints Commission. The organiser said the 'startlingly homophobic' piece is 'hardly acceptable as a piece of mainstream journalism.' Acceptable to whom? As with Julie Burchill, silencing people for the words they use when they have no other effect other than to offend is not the sign of a free country.

This chilling atmosphere extended even to legal practitioners themselves and into the lofty environs of the Law Society. Early in 2012, the organisation cancelled a discussion about marital break up because 'the programme reflected "an ethos which is opposed to same sex marriage"'. This was quite an extraordinary attempt to stifle legitimate debate on a matter which continues to polarise opinion. The organisers said that opposing gay marriage would be a breach of the country's equality laws, even though the practice had not even been legalised. Desmond Hudson, chief executive of the Law Society, said: 'We are proud of our role in promoting diversity in the solicitors' profession and felt that the content of this conference sat uncomfortably with our stance,' as if that justified what had happened.

In the past 12 months, two women have been sent to prison for making racist remarks on public transport that were recorded and then broadcast on YouTube. The complainants were not the immediate recipients of the abuse but people who watched the footage and found it offensive. At the very least, this raises questions about whether the prosecutions and the harsh penalties were justified. And yet, because the perpetrators used racist language hardly a peep has been heard to question the sentences. Anyone who suggests that the punishments were disproportionate is immediately identifying himself as a closet racist and BNP member. Yet there is something profoundly disturbing about the way these cases were handled and the absence of any public debate about them.

Jacqueline Woodhouse admitted she was drunk, as was evident from the film of her extended racist rant on a Tube train in January 2012, when she assailed passengers with her views about the presence of immigrants in this country. Woodhouse, from Romford in east London, boarded a packed Central Line train between St Paul's and Mile End stations and stumbled over a black woman named Judy Russell. She proceeded to hurl insults, shouting: 'You Africans take our council flats.' Her ensuing seven minute diatribe was videoed by another passenger who can be heard telling Woodhouse to keep her mouth shut and that she had drunk too much. 'It's not your country anyway so what's your problem?' she said. 'It's been overtaken by people like you.' In further remarks, she told passengers: 'I'll have you arrested because you don't live here' and 'I hope you are not claiming benefits.' The film was uploaded onto YouTube and complaints were made to British Transport Police by some of the 200,000 people who watched it.

Woodhouse handed herself into the police, telling officers she could not remember the comments but recognised herself in the video. She was charged with racially aggravated intentional harassment, to which she pleaded guilty at Westminster Magistrates Court.

Astonishingly, she was jailed for 21 weeks. Mr Juttla, of Ilford, east London, said: 'I found it very distressing. I uploaded it [the footage] to YouTube because I thought that was the fast-track process to catching this person. I also needed to show the public that kind of person is out there and not to put up with this kind of behaviour.'

Can this be right? Her behaviour was reprehensible but she was drunk and the people she abused seemed perfectly capable of sticking up for themselves. The court was told she threatened violence yet hardly seemed to be in any condition to stand up. In court, District Judge Michael Snow said: 'Anyone viewing it would feel a deep sense of shame that our citizens could be subject to such behaviour who may, as a consequence, believe that it secretly represents the views of other white people.'

But what if it does? Should it be a criminal offence to harbour bigoted opinions? The criminal justice system is not supposed to exist as a vehicle for people to parade their enlightened attitudes. Should the law be used to enforce a particular view of the world? Criminilisation is, after all, one of the most intrusive state interventions into the freedoms of the individual.

A similar fate befell another woman travelling on public transport, this time the tram between Mitcham and Wimbledon. Emma West was with her child in a push-chair, but this did not stop her launching into a racist diatribe against black people and eastern Europeans on the train.

A video was posted on YouTube in which she was heard to say 'What has this country come to? ... with loads of black people and load of f******g Polish.' You could equally ask what has this country come to when the criminal law is used against someone who not that long ago would have been dismissed as a sad case. Indeed she might well have been in this instance except that people who saw the video complained to the police. In line with the spirit of the times, West was arrested and charged with racially aggravated harassment and then held in custody for several weeks over Christmas, allegedly for her own safety.

It is extraordinary that she needed to rely upon activists from the BNP to say that this was wrong. She was also subject to psychiatric examination, presumably on the grounds that to harbour views that are considered unpalatable is a sign of madness. Holding people like West and Woodhouse up as martyrs to free speech is difficult. To categorise them in the same bracket as Socrates or Wilkes is clearly preposterous.

Yet there are parallels: they are being shut up and locked away for saying what they think, even if it is something that most people would consider the essence of bigotry. We have come a long way from a time when it was possible to say anything, however reprehensible, provided it did not seek to inspire violence or harm to others.

As a further sign of this new intolerance, when the West video was widely disseminated, people called for her deportation or her incarceration. We seem to have lost all sense of perspective where a rant on the Tube is considered justification for a prison sentence—ironically, often by the very people who argue that too many burglars or muggers or drug traffickers are sent to jail.

The law does have some locus in this area but its application must be proportionate to the offence. Who is to decide, after all, what tomorrow's outlandish view worthy of imprisonment is to be? Perhaps we are comfortable as a country with the law enforcing conformity to a set of beliefs and values judged to be acceptable. But we never used to be and it is not what made us a bastion of free speech. Can we really claim to be any longer?

Some people are always going to think hateful thoughts and say hateful things. In the past they have tended to express them to friends or others of a similar disposition. Occasionally, they have found an outlet in a political movement which has deliberately targeted minority ethnic or religious groups. They then become a threat to peace and order. But when they are the witterings of sad people captured on YouTube or disseminated via Twitter, the criminal law should not have a role to play.

As Josie Appleton incisively puts it: 'Hate speech regulation is an intervention into expressions of conflict or antagonism. It approaches political conflict as potentially explosive and destabilising, and recommends the state mediation of such conflict. This explains why hate speech regulation can encompass everything from extremely offensive to very mildly offensive speech.'[6]

She adds: 'Hate speech regulation curtails the moment of ideological conflict, when no crime has been committed. In this the state appears to be defending the victim. But it is actually defending itself, as the mediator and moderator of public debate, and the judge of what is and is not acceptable.'

It is not the job of the criminal law to penalise people for behaviour judged to be uncivil. And who is to judge? A view that today will attract arrest, for instance calling homosexuality a sin, was just a few decades ago supported by the law of the land.

The academic Jeremy Waldron maintains that 'legislative attention to hate speech is like environmental legislation; it seeks to preserve a very elementary aspect of the social environment against both sudden and slow-acting poisons of a particularly virulent kind.'[7] However, Timothy Garton Ash on his Free Speech Debate website argues that legislation on these matters is chilling and counter-productive, driving odious opinions underground and into the hands of extremists.[8]

'Living with difference is difficult,' he says. 'Our deeply cherished beliefs, values and ways of life do not merely contrast; they conflict. We should not be afraid of that. Conflict is an ineradicable part of freedom and a source of creativity. If there were no differences, we would have no choices and therefore no freedom. What we need is not to abolish conflict but to ensure that it happens in a civilised way.'

Garton Ash propounds a principle that 'as little as possible should be restricted by law, as much as possible regulated by our own free choices as grown-up neighbours, citizens and netizens.' He adds: 'Trying to impose civility by law has so many disadvantages. In the nature of something as complex as human identities in today's mixed-up world, it is very difficult to define exactly what should and should not be banned.'

For expression to remain free, says Garton Ash, we must have the right to offend; but that does not mean we have a duty to offend.

Yet defending free speech can mean sleeping with unsavoury bedfellows. Who would imagine, for instance, that John Terry would be seen as a martyr to free expression for firing off a string of expletives at a fellow footballer?

In June 2012, Terry, the former England soccer captain, was acquitted of causing racially aggravated harassment, alarm or distress under Section 5 of the Public Order Act 1986 and section 31 of the Crime and Disorder Act 1998. He is alleged to have called the QPR defender Anton Ferdinand a 'f*****g black c**t' during an altercation while playing for his club Chelsea.

In any sane world, such exchanges uttered in the heat of a sporting event would never be the subject of criminal charges but of internal disciplinary proceedings. Indeed, while Terry was found not guilty in court, where the burden of criminal proof is 'beyond reasonable doubt', he was subsequently found guilty at an FA disciplinary hearing where the charge had only to be proven on the balance of probabilities.

This trend became even more absurd when Chelsea Football Club laid allegations of racist language against the Premier League referee Mark Clattenburg for allegedly calling a black Nigerian footballer a 'monkey', and a Spanish player a 'Spanish twat', both of which he denied.

You would hope that referees do not go around the pitch swearing at players who seem perfectly able to deploy their own profanities. But Clattenburg was accused of something far worse than swearing: the use of racist language. It was speculated at the time that the referee might have deployed an idiomatic phrase that was lost in translation with so many foreign players on the pitch.

Of course words matter but the context is crucial, too. The conviction in November 2012 of a Welsh wedding guest for singing anti-English rugby songs on the bus home from the reception was an indication of how far down the slippery slope we have come. A law introduced to prevent the hate-filled abuse of vulnerable minorities is now being used to make people behave with decorum, something we used to police ourselves by telling the drunken oaf to shut up.

Instead, Phillip Pritchard of Swansea now has a criminal record for using racially aggravated threatening, insulting, abusive words or behaviour. And here is the rub: the complainant was not English but another Welshman 'who felt other people on the bus would take offence.' It is now possible, therefore, to be convicted of the serious offence of racial abuse even when the individual against whom it is aimed does not feel aggrieved.

Even more bizarre was the case of Petra Mills, who was found guilty of racially abusing her New Zealand-born neighbour Chelsea O'Reilly by calling her a 'stupid, fat Australian'. Ms O'Reilly said: 'She knew I was from New Zealand. She was trying to be offensive. I was really insulted.' Judge Brian Donohue agreed: 'The word Australian was used. It was racially aggravated and the main reason it was used was in hostility.' He fined Mills £110 for racially aggravated public disorder. How is it possible for a race hate offence to continue being used in this way without bringing the entire law into disrepute? If this is the price we have to pay to enforce good behaviour and create social harmony, it is too high.

Conclusion

Belatedly, prosecutors are trying to come to terms in law with the stupidity of some people and the ease with which their idiocies can be disseminated. In December 2012, Keir Starmer, the Director of Public Prosecutions, issued new guidelines on when and if to bring charges against people leaving offensive remarks on social media sites.[1]

These sought to draw a clear distinction between cases that constitute a credible threat of violence, stalking, harassment or a breach of a court order—clearly requiring robust prosecution in the public interest—and those cases characterised as unpopular, or even very offensive comments, which often will not.

But in that case, why is the same distinction not drawn when people talk directly to each other? Why is it different when filtered through a social media site? This approach could leave us in the ludicrous position where saying something in public will fall foul of the law yet tweeting an identical comment will be allowed.

We have far too many laws in this area circumscribing free speech—not just the hate crimes of Labour or the Public Order Acts but also the Communications Act 2003 and the Malicious Communications Act 1988. The police and prosecutors move from one to the other to close down views they deem to be unacceptable.

As Starmer said: 'Whatever view one may take on the reach of the criminal law, the CPS must decide whether or not to bring charges against an individual who may have committed an offence under the law as it stands, which is why the new guidelines are so important—they are designed to ensure a consistency of approach to such decisions across the CPS.'

Starmer made this point himself: 'The right to freedom of expression covers not only speech which is well-received and popular, but also that which is offensive, shocking or disturbing. Just because content in a communication is in bad taste, controversial or unpopular, and may cause offences to individuals or a specific community, that is not in itself sufficient reason to put someone through the court process. Only where content is so grossly offensive that it can be considered well over the line—beyond that which is tolerable in an open and diverse society—should prosecutors consider bringing charges.'

Other factors should also be taken into account where social media abuse is concerned, including swift action to take down the offending message, the intention of the sender and their age and maturity. Prosecutions should be a proportionate response not an automatic response. Again, surely this approach should apply to the drunk on the train shouting abuse at people or to the funda-mentalist in the street questioning the morality of homo-sexuality?

What we need now, however, are not more guidelines that will confuse matters further but a wholesale review to bring some consistency to all these laws while highlighting the freedom of speech protections that Parliament has passed. For centuries we have sought to establish the appropriate boundary between the legitimate expectation of people not to suffer offensive insults and the right to freedom of expression. We have not got it right yet.

Notes

Preface

1   Chevenix Trench, C., *Portrait of a Patriot: a biography of John Wilkes*, London 1962.

Introduction:

1   HC Deb, 5 July 2005, c399W.

2   *Guardian* website, January 2013.

3   *Telegraph* website, 15 January 2013.

1: The Retreat of Free Speech

1   Appleton, J., 'There ain't no harm in hate speech', *Spiked Online*, October 2012.

2   Appleton, 'There ain't no harm in hate speech', 2012.

2: The Trial of Socrates

1   Stone, I.F., *The Trial of Socrates*, Jonathan Cape, 1988, p. 212.

2   Webster, R., *Reconsidering the Rushdie Affair: Freedom, censorship and American foreign policy*, 1992.

3   *Independent*, 31 January 1997.

4   *Daily Telegraph*, 3 October 2008.

5   O'Neill, B., *Spiked,* 13 January 2010.

6   O'Neill, *Spiked,* 13 January 2010.

3: Protecting Public Order

1   HC Deb, 16 November 1936, vol. 317, cc1349-473.

2   HC Deb, 16 November 1936, vol. 317, cc1349-473.

3   HC Deb, 13 January 1986, vol. 89, cc792-869.

4   His Honour Judge Peter Thornton QC, *et al*, *The Law of Public Order and Protest*, 2010, Oxford University Press, p. 36.

5   Editorial, *The Times*, 7 December 1985.

6   Editorial, *Daily Telegraph*, 7 December 1985.

7   *Consultation on Police Powers to Promote and Maintain Public Order*, JUSTICE Consultation Response, January 2012, para. 5; http://www.justice.org.uk/data/files/resources/316/Microso ft-Word-JUSTICE-Police-Powers-Protest-Response-Jan-2012-FINAL.pdf

8   Harvey *v* DPP, Royal Courts of Justice, 17 November 2011.

9   *Consultation on Police Powers to Promote and Maintain Public Order*, JUSTICE Consultation Response, January 2012, paras 10 and 11;

http://www.justice.org.uk/data/files/resources/316/Microso ft-Word-JUSTICE-Police-Powers-Protest-Response-Jan-2012-FINAL.pdf

10   HL Deb, 9 July 2009, c802.

11   Comment is Free, *Guardian*, 6 October 2009.

12   Racial and Religious Hatred Act, 2006, Section 29J.

13   *Pink News*, 19 March 2009.

14   HL Deb, 9 July 2009, c802.

4: Case Studies

1   Sharon Vogelenzang written evidence to the Protection of Freedom Bill committee, March 2011.

2   *Daily Mail*, 10 December 2009.

3   House of Commons committee on the Protection of Freedom Bill; http://www.publications.parliament.uk/pa/cm201011/cmpublic/protection/memo/pf7.htm

4   *Daily Mail*, 10 December 2009.

5   House of Commons committee on the Protection of Freedom Bill; http://www.publications.parliament.uk/pa/cm201011/cmpublic/protection/memo/pf7.htm

6   *Daily Mail*, 20 September 2009.

7   BBC News website, 23 May 2008.

8   BBC News Website, 22 March 2006.

9   *This is Worcestershire,* 11 March 2006.

10   *Northern Echo,* 27 April 2007.

11   *Northern Echo,* 27 April 2007.

12   BBC, 12 January 2006.

13   *Guardian,* 18 January 2012.

14   *Hansard,* 23 March 2011. Memorandum submitted to the Commons committee into the Protections of Freedom Bill, 23 March 2011; http://www.publications.parliament.uk/pa/cm201011/cmpublic/protection/memo/pf12.htm

15   *Hansard,* 23 March 2011. Memorandum submitted to the Commons committee into the Protections of Freedom Bill, 23 March 2011; http://www.publications.parliament.uk/pa/cm201011/cmpublic/protection/memo/pf12.htm

5: What Happened to Common Law Protections?

1 Redmond-Bate *v* Director of Public Prosecutions 163 JP 789, [1999] Crim LR 998, 7 BHRC 375 QUEEN'S BENCH DIVISION SEDLEY LJ, COLLINS J, 23 July 1999.

2 *The Lawyer*, 9 June 1999.

3 Redmond-Bate *v* Director of Public Prosecutions 163 JP 789, [1999] Crim LR 998, 7 BHRC 375 QUEEN'S BENCH DIVISION SEDLEY LJ, COLLINS J, 23 July 1999.

4 *Keeping the Peace*, ACPO, 2010, chapter 2.27 etc.

5 *Keeping the Peace*, ACPO, 2010, chapter 2.46.

6 *Hansard*, c1118W, HC written answers, 20 December 2010.

7 *Guardian*, 18 January 2012.

8 *Conservativehome* blog, 4 July 2012.

9 See CPS website: Crown Prosecution Service, Public Order Offences incorporating the Charging Standard; http://www.cps.gov.uk/legal/p_to_r/public_order_offences/#Section_5

10 *Hansard* , Col. 1121, House of Lords debates 12 December 2012.

11 Percy *v* DPP [1995] Crim LR 714.

12 Redmond-Bate *v* DPP (1999) 163 JP 789.

13 Judge Peter Thornton QC, *et al*, *The Law of Public Order and Protest*, 2010, p. 36.

6: Free Speech in the Age of Twitter and YouTube

1 *Guardian*, 11 May 2010.

2 *Guardian*, 11 May 2010.

3 Hitchens, C., Speech in Hart House, University of Toronto, 15 November 2006.

4 *Guardian*, 27 March 2012; http://www.guardian.co.uk/uk/2012/mar/27/student-jailed-fabrice-muamba-tweets

5 *Guardian*, 27 July 2012.

6 Appleton, J., 'There ain't no harm in hate speech', *Spiked Online*, October 2012.

7 Free Speech Debate, 20 March 2012.

8 Freespeechdebate.idebate.org

Conclusion

1 See CPS website: Interim guidelines on prosecuting cases involving communications sent via social media; http://www.cps.gov.uk/consultations/social_media_consultation.html